Dr. Patricia Green

THE SEVEN SPIRITS
of YAHWEH

Copyright © 2014 by Dr. Patricia Green

All rights reserved. No part of this book may be used, reproduced, stored in a retrieval system, or transmitted in any form whatsoever — including electronic, photocopy, recording — without prior written permission from the author, except in the case of brief quotations embodied in critical articles or reviews.

All scripture quotations, unless otherwise indicated, are taken from the *Holy Bible, New King James Version*, Copyright © 1982 by Thomas Nelson, Inc.

Additional Scripture quotations are taken from the *Hebraic Roots Bible*, Copyright 2012 by Word of Truth Publications.

Cover Design by Prophetic Artist James Nesbit www.jamesnart.net

SECOND EDITION

ISBN: 978-1-939748-54-6

Library of Congress Control Number: 2014935209

Published by

P.O. Box 2839, Apopka, FL 32703

Printed in the United States of America

Dedication

This book is dedicated to

My Papa YAHWEH
and
My Precious Savior YAHSHUA

You alone are Almighty and All Powerful
and Your Name is an Everlasting Name.

You are the Lion of the Tribe of Judah.

I love you with a passion that overflows from my
heart like a majestic waterfall pouring over
the rocks with the mist of the latter rain.

Table Of Contents

NOTE: In this book I will use God the Father's Hebrew name, Yahweh; and Jesus' Hebrew name, Yahshua. It is important for me to honor Yahweh and Yahshua by calling them by their true names. The Bible quotes used in this book are from the New King James Version and do not contain their real Hebrew names.

Introduction

We are living in extremely exciting times where biblical prophecies are being fulfilled and the signs that were spoken of by Yahshua are upon us. More than ever, the body of Christ needs the fullness of the Seven Spirits of Yahweh to be spiritually strong in these last days. The fact that you are reading this book, says you are hungry for the deeper things of Yahweh and you are seeking His truth.

In order to understand the Seven Spirits of Yahweh, I need to expose an erroneous teaching that has been widely accepted by most mainstream Protestant churches. Martin Luther, who broke away from Catholicism, was the pioneer of the Protest Movement we know as Protestantism. All Protestant churches today have their roots in Catholicism and we have inherited some doctrines that originated in the Catholic Church. I know because I was raised as a Catholic and attended a Catholic school; but now I am a born-again Spirit-filled follower and lover of Yahshua. The erroneous doctrine I want to expose that has filtered down through Catholicism is the trinity. I am not saying there is not Father, Son, and Holy Spirit. Scriptures shows us there is much more to the fullness of Yahweh than the trinity teaching. Before you hang me out to dry and label me a heretic, take your dogmatic doctrine you have been taught in the past and place it on a shelf until you finish this book.

Through the residue of Catholicism that followed into Protestantism, we have been taught that God is three persons in one and they are equal in power and yet distinct and separate in their function. The trinity is a misleading teaching that does not address the scriptures which reveal the Seven Spirits of Yahweh. You will not find this teaching in most mainstream denominational churches because they have been influenced by Catholic doctrine, whether they want to admit it or not.

Constantine promoted the trinity as a way to unite his kingdom under one religion. He decreed that everyone in his kingdom must convert to Christianity, which became a problem for the pagans who worshipped many deities. By promoting the trinity doctrine, Constantine inoculated the pagans and the Christians with partial truth which concealed the power of the Seven Spirits of Yahweh. He was able to unite his kingdom because the pagans could accept a religion where there were multiple gods and the Christians could celebrate their trinity. The pagans added the three Gods of the trinity to their many gods and called themselves Christians and everyone was happy. Everyone accept Yahweh. In these last days, Yahweh's truth will prevail about His Seven Spirits and the importance of being immersed into the fullness of His Spirits.

In order to undo the indoctrination of the trinity, we must examine the basis for all truth and that is the Holy Scriptures. There are several scriptures that unveil the Seven Spirits of Yahweh because His Word reveals truth. Have you ever been driving in thick fog in the early morning and it begins to lift? When the heavy fog lifts, the beautiful lush valley can be seen, and then the backdrop of the majestic mountains, and finally the crystal blue heavens. There is a sequence when the fog lifts. First you see the green valley below, then you see the towering mountains, and last you see the beautiful heavens. When the fog from confusing teaching is lifted step by step through the truth of His Word, one can clearly see the very things that were hidden. Journey with me into the glorious heavens, for that which was hidden is now being revealed.

Zechariah was awakened by an angel and the angel asked him what he saw. Zechariah replied, "I am looking, and there is a lampstand of solid gold with a bowl on top of it, and on the stand seven lamps with seven pipes to the seven lamps" (Zechariah 4:2). After questioning Zechariah about what he saw, the angel reported to Zechariah that Zerubbabel would build the second temple and many would rejoice over it. Yahweh was intently focused on this new temple and He was jubilant because this would be the temple that His Son Yahshua would be dedicated in. Then this angel gave us the first glimpse of the Seven Spirits of Yahweh when he said the seven lamps are the seven eyes of Yahweh.

> "For these seven rejoice to see
> The plumb line in the hand of Zerubbabel.
> They are the eyes of the Lord,
> Which scan to and fro throughout the whole earth."
> (Zechariah 4:10)

The angel also gave us another clue about these seven eyes which are Seven Spirits of Yahweh. He said that these seven eyes or seven lamps of Yahweh are scanning throughout the entire earth. What are the Seven Spirits of Yahweh looking for on this earth and how are they connected to man?

"For His eyes are on the ways of man,
And He sees all his steps." (Job 34:21)
The spirit of a man is the lamp of the Lord,
Searching all the inner depths of his heart." (Proverbs 20:27)

Scripture indicates that the eyes of Yahweh are upon us and through our spirits; Yahweh has access to our hearts. In other words, the Seven Spirits of Yahweh knows exactly what is in the hearts of all people. When He finds one who loves Him and is loyal, His Seven Spirits are drawn towards that person so He can impart His strength.

"For the eyes of the Lord run to and fro throughout the whole earth, to show Himself strong on behalf of those whose heart is loyal to Him." (2 Chronicles 16:9)

In the Book of Revelation, these seven lamps and seven eyes are also identified as the Seven Spirits of Yahweh. The Apostle John was lifted up in the spirit to the third heaven and was given a view of the throne of Yahweh. John understood that these seven lamps of fire and the seven eyes were the Seven Spirits of Yahweh. More importantly, he understood that these Seven Spirits of Yahweh were sent out into all the earth.

"And from the throne proceeded lightnings, thunderings, and voices. Seven lamps of fire were burning before the throne, which are the seven Spirits of God." (Revelation 4:5)

"And I looked, and behold, in the midst of the throne and of the four living creatures, and in the midst of the elders, stood a Lamb as though it had been slain, having seven horns and seven eyes, which the seven Spirits of God are sent out into all the earth." (Revelation 5:6)

On my first trip to Malawi I had a divine appointment with some pastors and prophets who were gathered for prayer. We were all praying in the Spirit and the manifest presence of Holy Spirit permeated the atmosphere. A prophet from Malawi began to reveal what he had just seen in a vision. He said, "Dr. Patricia, I just saw you in a vision. You were standing on a large rock and you were wearing a full suit of armor. When you spoke, fire came out of your mouth. In your right hand were seven arrows. You are one of God's end time warrior's and you are on the front line of battle." I understood the meaning of the vision with the exception of the seven arrows. At first I thought they represented seven African nations I would evangelize and preach in. Two years later when I returned to Malawi, Holy Spirit revealed to me what the seven arrows represented. He instructed me to go to Revelation 4:5 and Isaiah 11:1-2.

"And from the throne proceeded lightnings, thunderings, and voices. Seven lamps of fire were burning before the throne, which are the seven Spirits of God." (Revelation 4:5)

"There shall come forth a Rod from the stem of Jesse,
And a Branch shall grow out of his roots.
The Spirit of the Lord shall rest upon Him,
The Spirit of wisdom and understanding,
The Spirit of counsel and might,
The Spirit of knowledge and of the
fear of the Lord." (Isaiah 11:1-2)

Immediately upon reading these scriptures, I knew that Isaiah had identified the Seven Spirits of Yahweh written about in Revelation. I could see from this scripture that these Seven Spirits of Yahweh rested upon Yahshua.

The Spirit of Yahweh

The Spirit of Wisdom

The Spirit of Understanding

The Spirit of Counsel

The Spirit of Might

The Spirit of Knowledge

The Spirit of the Fear of Yahweh

The words spoken by the angel to Joshua the high priest also corroborate that the seven eyes are the Seven Spirits of Yahweh that rested on Yahshua, the Branch.

'Hear, O Joshua, the high priest,

You and your companions who sit before you,

For they are a wondrous sign;

For behold, I am bringing forth My Servant the BRANCH.

For behold, the stone

That I have laid before Joshua:

Upon the stone are seven eyes.

Behold, I will engrave its inscription,

Says the Lord of hosts,

And I will remove the iniquity of that

land in one day." (Zechariah 3:8-9)

After I received these revelations from scripture through His Spirit, Yahweh began to speak to me about the vision that was given to the prophet in Malawi. *"Patricia, those seven arrows in your right hand are My Seven Spirits and I have imparted them to you. If My Son, Yahshua needed My Seven Spirits to operate in signs, wonders, and miracles while He was on earth, then how much more do you need them? Impart My Seven Spirits to empower people to operate in signs, wonders, and miracles."*

I began to impart the Seven Spirits of Yahweh to those who already had the Baptism of Holy Spirit. Through prayer and studying scriptures, Holy Spirit revealed to me that the Baptism of Holy Spirit and the Seven Spirits of Yahweh are two different gifts of grace. John the Baptist was baptizing in water for the repentance of sin when he said this. "I indeed baptize you with water unto repentance, but He who is coming after me is mightier than I, whose sandals I am not worthy to carry. He will baptize you with the Holy Spirit and fire" (Matthew 3:11). John the Baptist stated that Yahshua would baptize with Holy Spirit and baptize with fire. The Baptism of Holy Spirit is one baptism and the Baptism of fire is another baptism.

In the Baptism of Holy Spirit, the spiritual gifts are imparted and then the gifts begin to outwardly manifest as you utilize them. They become evident through speaking in tongues, words of knowledge, and words of wisdom, prophetic words, discerning spirits and casting them out, healing the sick, interpreting messages in tongues, having supernatural faith, and witnessing miracles. Being baptized by the Seven Lamps of Fire which are the Seven Spirits of Yahweh takes one to a higher spiritual level to do kingdom work. This is not about receiving more power for the sake of manifesting power. This is about being empowered with signs, wonders, and miracles to storm the gates of hell and declare the kingdom of Yahweh is at hand. This is about getting people birthed into His kingdom and set free from the works of the enemy. This baptism is for greater power through the Seven Spirits of Yahweh and comes through an impartation. This impartation allows you to enter into the fullness of His Seven Spirits. In the Book of Acts, Paul received an impartation when Ananias laid hands on him.

> "And Ananias went his way and entered the house; and laying his hands on him he said, 'Brother Saul, the Lord Jesus, who appeared to you on the road as you came, has sent me that you may receive your sight and be filled with the Holy Spirit.'" (Acts 9:17)

The first place I imparted the Seven Spirits of Yahweh was in Malawi, the place I was given the vision. Then I began teaching and imparting the Seven Spirits of Yahweh in the USA to a number of people. I imparted the Seven Spirits of Yahweh to a minister in Virginia and like many I have ministered to, this impartation was new to him. After he heard me teach on the subject, it answered a long standing question he had about the Seven Spirits of God in the book of Revelation. When he received the impartation, he quickly noticed an increase in his spiritual power for healing, discerning of spirits, and much more. Two weeks after he was immersed into the Seven Spirits of Yahweh, he attended a service where an Apostle from Nigeria was preaching. This Apostle taught on the Seven Spirits of Yahweh and the minister from Virginia was amazed to hear the exact same teaching that I had given him just two weeks previous. This Apostle from Nigeria was adamant that he does not permit any of his leaders to minister unless they receive the fullness of the Seven Spirits of Yahweh. One thousand pastors in Nigeria have received this impartation because this Apostle has established one thousand churches in his country. He holds a government position and was appointed by President Goodluck Jonathan to oversee the spiritual welfare of Nigeria. Nigeria is blessed to have a President who a is born-again believer in Yahshua and blessed to have an Apostle imparting the Seven Spirits of Yahweh.

This book is about teaching people the truth about the fullness of the Seven Spirits of Yahweh. There is no doubt that our heavenly Father is named Yahweh and our Savior is named Yahshua. There is also no doubt that the Seven Spirits of Yahweh have much to convey to us, as we quickly approach the last days before Yahshua returns. There is much work to be done to reap this great end time harvest of souls and one of my tasks is to impart the Seven Spirits of Yahweh to you. It is time for the sons and daughters of Yahweh to be true disciples of Yahshua who operate in the fullness of the Seven Spirits of Yahweh, openly declaring His majesty through signs, wonders, and miracles!

CHAPTER ONE

The Spirit of Yahweh

The Spirit of Yahweh spoke this message so we could understand Him in a fresh way. *"I AM the brightest Light in the universe. The sun is but a shadow of My brightness. In My Presence, darkness does not exist. My Light is the sustainer of all life. I AM the Healing Light. When a person's spirit becomes born again by My Spirit, they have My Light. Those who have My Spirit radiate My Light and the closer they are to Me, the brighter the light. In the spiritual realm, the angels can see your light and the demons can see your light. The enemy flees from the brightness of My Light which is upon you and in you. You carry My Light wherever you go."*

Yahshua came as the Light of Yahweh, but before He ascended into heaven, he made a promise to His disciples that He would enable them to be the light of the world. This could only happen through the Spirit of Yahweh. The Spirit of Yahweh is Holy Spirit and His Hebrew name is Ruach haKodesh. In the Book of Acts, Yahshua instructed His disciples to remain in Jerusalem because they would be immersed or baptized into Holy Spirit. Although they did not understand Yahshua's orders, one hundred and twenty obeyed His directive and remained in Jerusalem. They gathered in an upper room and fervently prayed in unity. They were assembled together on the day of Pentecost, which is the 50th day after the Passover, when suddenly there was the sound of a roaring wind. The rushing wind was an outward sign that a portal to heaven was opened, through which the Spirit of Yahweh made a divine visitation. His Holy Presence came as fire which rested upon the occupants of the house.

The Spirit of Yahweh filled each person with His power so they would be equipped to take the gospel to the ends of the earth. They received all of the spiritual gifts that were later written about by Paul in his first letter to the Corinthians. These spiritual gifts were necessary to fulfill Yahweh's plans for His disciples. Through the Spirit of Yahweh, the fearful disciples became bold and their tongues were loosed to speak in languages they did not learn or know. They were compelled to speak in other tongues and proclaim the wonders of Yahweh to all those who were gathered in Jerusalem for the feast of Pentecost. This wondrous phenomenon was the remedy to the confusion of tongues Yahweh caused at the tower of Babel. The curse was reversed because Yahweh wanted the good news about His Son's redemption made known to every nation. This good news about Yahshua was no longer just for the house of Israel, it was for the entire world.

The Spirit of Yahweh is Power. Power is authority. Power is supremacy. Power is influence. Power is clout. Power is rule. The Spirit of Yahweh gives us authority over sin, sickness, and the oppression of Satan and his minions. The Spirit of Yahweh has given us supremacy over the powers of darkness because they were defeated when Yahshua retrieved the keys of hades and death. The Spirit of Yahweh supernaturally imparts His power so we can successfully live according to His Word and influence others. Without His Holy Spirit, we cannot overcome our flesh, overcome the enticement of the world, or overcome the attacks of evil spirits. The Spirit of Yahweh gives us clout because we are seated in the heavenly realm with Yahshua. We carry the power of the Spirit of Yahweh which establishes His rule through us on this earth. He gave us dominion of this planet which means to rule over its entire domain. This all may sound lofty, but on the contrary, this is for everyone who has the power of the Spirit of Yahweh! The only way to have His power is to receive Him through the Baptism into Holy Spirit, just like the disciples received His power. "But you shall receive power when the Holy Spirit has come upon you; and you shall be witnesses to Me in Jerusalem, and in all Judea and Samaria, and to the end of the earth" (Acts 1:8). If you want the Baptism of Holy Spirit, you can receive it at the end of this book, but continue reading so you can be prepared to receive.

It is through the power of Yahweh that we overcome the schemes and tactics of Satan. Satan and his demons have one goal and that is to kill, steal and destroy those who belong to Yahweh. There was a season in my life when the enemy was attacking my joints and my muscles with excruciating chronic pain. I was desperately seeking Yahweh and Yahshua and asking for answers. I was praying one morning and Yahweh spoke His words to my spirit. *"Though your body may be afflicted with pain this day, do not despair, for I am about to deliver you."*

A few days after receiving His message, I was awakened at 12:30 AM with another reflective message from the Spirit of Yahweh. He said to me: *"I AM everything the Word says that I AM."* Immediately my mind went to the encounter Moses had at the burning bush. Yahweh appeared to Moses as fire that did not consume; the identical fire He appeared to the disciples in the upper room.

> "And God said to Moses, "I AM WHO I AM." And He said, "Thus you shall say to the children of Israel, 'I AM has sent me to you." (Exodus 3:14)

Yahweh identified Himself to Moses as "I AM" and He identified Himself to me in the middle of the night as "I AM." When I contemplated His message, *"I AM everything the Word says that I AM,"* I knew Yahweh was giving me heart knowledge that He and His Word are inseparable and everything written in scriptures is irrefutable truth. In the midst of my pain, Yahweh wanted me to know that His Word cannot return to Him empty or void. He was reassuring me that He was going to deliver me from this physical pain because His Word promises deliverance from pain and disease.

There is a difference between having intellectual knowledge of the Word of God and having heart knowledge. Intellectual knowledge is acquired because you have studied a subject or read about it. Heart knowledge is attained because Holy Spirit has brought revelation to your spirit. Many people have head knowledge *about* the Word of God, but they need to have heart knowledge *through* the sword of the Spirit of Yahweh. The best way to attain heart knowledge of scriptures is to pray in the Spirit while studying and reading His Word.

The second heart knowledge fact that Holy Spirit wanted me to know is that everything stated in the Word about me is truth. This truth is backed up by the Great "I AM." When this revelation went from my mind to my spirit, biblical truths flowed from my pen as fast as I could write. I rapidly wrote these statements and when I was done I was surprised to count forty. Forty is the number of testing and I knew I was in a desert place of testing.

Everyone who knows Yahshua as Lord and Savior can be transformed by these "I AM" truths I wrote. The Spirit of Yahweh desires to minister to you through His Word. Your body will begin to heal. Your soul will be refreshed and bondage from emotional wounds will be healed. Your spirit will soar to new heights and you will press deeper into Him. I urge you to read these next forty statements out loud along with the scriptures. They will establish His Word and His Spirit in your life so you can boldly proclaim, "I AM everything the Word says that I AM."

I AM saved by grace through my faith in Yahshua and born again by Yahweh's Spirit.

> "For by grace you have been saved through faith, and that not of yourselves; it is the gift of God, not of works, lest anyone should boast." (Ephesians 2:8-9)

> "Jesus answered and said to him, "Most assuredly, I say to you, unless one is born again, he cannot see the kingdom of God." (John 3:3)

I AM recorded in the Lambs Book of Life and my name is written in heaven.

> "Nevertheless do not rejoice in this, that the spirits are subject to you, but rather rejoice because your names are written in heaven." (Luke 20:10)

> "And I saw the dead, small and great, standing before God, and books were opened. And another book was opened, which is the Book of Life. And the dead were judged

according to their works, by the things which were written in the books." (Revelation 20:10)

I AM healed from every disease, sickness, infirmity, and pain because of the finished work Yahshua accomplished on the cross.

> "Who Himself bore our sins in His own body on the tree, that we, having died to sins, might live for righteousness— by whose stripes you were healed." (1 Peter 2:24)

> "He sent His word and healed them." (Psalm 107:20)

> "Bless the Lord, O my soul,
> And forget not all His benefits:
> Who forgives all your iniquities,
> Who heals all your diseases." (Psalm 103:2-3)

I AM delivered from the power of Satan and all demonic influence.

> "In order to turn them from darkness to light, and from the power of Satan to God, that they may receive forgiveness of sins and an inheritance among those who are sanctified by faith in Me." (Acts 26:17-18)

> "Therefore submit to God. Resist the devil and he will flee from you." (James 4:7)

I AM forgiven of all my sins and iniquities.

> "You have forgiven the iniquity of Your people; You have covered all their sin." (Psalm 85:2)

> "But that you may know that the Son of Man has power on

earth to forgive sins"—then He said to the paralytic, "Arise, take up your bed, and go to your house." (Matthew 9:6)

I AM victorious over all sin because sin no longer has dominion over me.

> "For sin shall not have dominion over you, for you are not under law but under grace. And having been set free from sin, you became slaves of righteousness." (Romans 6:14, 18)

I AM loved as a son or daughter by my Papa Yahweh.

> "For you are all sons of God through faith in Christ Jesus. And because you are sons, God has sent forth the Spirit of His Son into your hearts, crying out, "Abba, Father!" (Galatians 3:26, 4:6)

> "For you did not receive the spirit of bondage again to fear, but you received the Spirit of adoption by whom we cry out, "Abba, Father." The Spirit Himself bears witness with our spirit that we are children of God." (Romans 8:15-16)

I AM inscribed in the palms of Yahweh and no one can pluck me out of His hand.

> "See, I have inscribed you on the palms of My hands." (Isaiah 49:16)

> "My Father, who has given them to Me, is greater than all; and no one is able to snatch them out of My Father's hand." (John 10:29)

I AM a new creation in Christ because He is in me and I am in Him and we are one.

> "Therefore, if anyone is in Christ, he is a new creation; old things have passed away; behold, all things have become new." (2 Corinthians 5:17)

> "I do not pray for these alone, but also for those who will believe in Me through their word; that they all may be one, as You, Father, are in Me, and I in You; that they also may be one in Us, that the world may believe that You sent Me. And the glory which You gave Me I have given them, that they may be one just as We are one." (John 17:20-22)

I AM perfectly righteous in the eyes of Yahweh because of my faith in Yahshua.

> "That I may gain Christ and be found in Him, not having my own righteousness, which is from the law, but that which is through faith in Christ, the righteousness which is from God by faith." (Philippians 3:9-10)

I AM seated in heavenly places in Christ because I am a joint heir with Him.

> "And if children, then heirs—heirs of God and joint heirs with Christ, if indeed we suffer with Him, that we may also be glorified together." (Romans 8:17)

> "Made us alive together with Christ (by grace you have been saved), and raised us up together, and made us sit together in the heavenly places in Christ Jesus." (Ephesians 2:5-6)

I AM holy as He is holy and I have His power to make right choices and to walk in holiness.

> "But as He who called you is holy, you also be holy in all your conduct, because it is written, "Be holy, for I am holy." (1 Peter 1:15-16)

> "But now having been set free from sin, and having become slaves of God, you have your fruit to holiness, and the end, everlasting life." (Romans 6:22)

I AM strong in Christ and able to accomplish all things through Him.

> "I can do all things through Christ who strengthens me." (Philippians 4:13)

I AM absolutely Yahshua's possession because He bought me with a precious price.

> "For if we live, we live to the Lord; and if we die, we die to the Lord. Therefore, whether we live or die, we are the Lord's." (Romans 14:8)

> "For you were bought at a price; therefore glorify God in your body and in your spirit, which are God's." (1 Corinthians 6:20)

I AM a temple of Yahweh because His Spirit lives in me.

> "Do you not know that you are the temple of God and that the Spirit of God dwells in you? If anyone defiles the temple of God, God will destroy him. For the temple of

God is holy, which temple you are." (1 Corinthians 3:16-17)

I AM crucified with Christ and I no longer live for my selfish desires because He lives in me.

> "I have been crucified with Christ; it is no longer I who live, but Christ lives in me; and the life which I now live in the flesh I live by faith in the Son of God, who loved me and gave Himself for me." (Galatians 2:20)

I AM complete in Yahshua because He will finish the work He began in me the day I gave my life to Him.

> "Being confident of this very thing, that He who has begun a good work in you will complete it until the day of Jesus Christ." (Philippians 1:6)

I AM created to worship, praise, and thank Yahweh and Yahshua.

> "That at the name of Jesus every knee should bow, of those in heaven, and of those on earth, and of those under the earth, and that every tongue should confess that Jesus Christ is Lord, to and the glory of God the Father." (Philippians 2:10-11)

> "In everything give thanks; for this is the will of God in Christ Jesus for you." (1 Thessalonians 5:18)

I AM an ambassador for Christ and I am His representative in my hometown, my state, my country and the nations.

> "That utterance may be given to me, that I may open my mouth boldly to make known the mystery of the gospel, for

which I am an ambassador in chains; that in it I may speak boldly, as I ought to speak." (Ephesians 6:19-20)

"You shall be witnesses to Me in Jerusalem, and in all Judea and Samaria, and to the end of the earth." (Acts 1:8)

I AM sanctified or set apart to do good works by laying hands on the sick so they shall recover.

"For we are His workmanship, created in Christ Jesus for good works, which God prepared beforehand that we should walk in them." (Ephesians 2:10)

"They will take up serpents; and if they drink anything deadly, it will by no means hurt them; they will lay hands on the sick, and they will recover." (Mark 16:18)

I AM prosperous because He provides all my needs.

"And my God shall supply all your need according to His riches in glory by Christ Jesus." (Philippians 4:19)

"Beloved, I pray that you may prosper in all things and be in health, just as your soul prospers." (3 John 1:2)

I AM protected under Yahweh's wings and protected by His angels.

"He who dwells in the secret place of the Most High
Shall abide under the shadow of the Almighty.
He shall cover you with His feathers,
And under His wings you shall take refuge.
For He shall give His angels charge over you,
To keep you in all your ways." (Psalm 91:1, 4, 11)

"Are they not all ministering spirits sent forth to minister for those who will inherit salvation?" (Hebrews 1:14)

I AM mentally sound and able to make decisions according to His will because I have the mind of Christ.

> "For God has not given us a spirit of fear, but of power and of love and of a sound mind." (2 Timothy 2:7)

> "And do not be conformed to this world, but be transformed by the renewing of your mind, that you may prove what *is* that good and acceptable and perfect will of God." (Romans 12:2)

> "Let this mind be in you which was also in Christ Jesus." (Philippians 2:5)

I AM able to perform signs, wonders and miracles which will accompany the preaching of the Gospel message.

> "And He said to them, "Go into all the world and preach the gospel to every creature. He who believes and is baptized will be saved; but he who does not believe will be condemned. And these signs will follow those who believe: In My name they will cast out demons; they will speak with new tongues; they will take up serpents; and if they drink anything deadly, it will by no means hurt them; they will lay hands on the sick, and they will recover." (Mark 16:15-18)

> "For our gospel did not come to you in word only, but also in power, and in the Holy Spirit." (1 Thessalonians 1:5)

I AM immersed into His Spirit and I have the fullness of Yahweh's Seven Spirits.

> "But you shall receive power when the Holy Spirit has come upon you." (Acts 1:8)

> "The Spirit of the Lord shall rest upon Him,
> The Spirit of wisdom and understanding,
> The Spirit of counsel and might,
> The Spirit of knowledge and of the
> fear of the Lord." (Isaiah 11:2)

I AM full of faith to move mountains of adversity because Yahshua is the Author and Finisher of my faith.

> "So Jesus answered and said to them, "Assuredly, I say to you, if you have faith and do not doubt, you will not only do what was done to the fig tree, but also if you say to this mountain, 'Be removed and be cast into the sea,' it will be done." (Matthew 21:21)

> "Looking unto Jesus, the author and finisher of our faith, who for the joy that was set before Him endured the cross, despising the shame, and has sat down at the right hand of the throne of God." (Hebrews 12:2)

I AM called by Yahshua to be an Apostle, Shepherd, Teacher, Evangelist, or Prophet filled with all spiritual gifts which are given to me by my Father in heaven.

> "And He Himself gave some to be apostles, some prophets, some evangelists, and some pastors and teachers, for the

equipping of the saints for the work of ministry, for the edifying of the body of Christ." (Ephesians 4:11-12)

"But the manifestation of the Spirit is given to each one for the profit of all: for to one is given the word of wisdom through the Spirit, to another the word of knowledge through the same Spirit, to another faith by the same Spirit, to another gifts of healings by the same Spirit, to another the working of miracles, to another prophecy, to another discerning of spirits, to another different kinds of tongues, to another the interpretation of tongues. But one and the same Spirit works all these things, distributing to each one individually as He wills." (1 Corinthians 12:7-11)

I AM a warrior dressed in the full armor of Yahweh and I am on the front line of battle against the gates of hell.

"Put on the whole armor of God, that you may be able to stand against the wiles of the devil. Stand therefore, having girded your waist with truth, having put on the breastplate of righteousness, and having shod your feet with the preparation of the gospel of peace; above all, taking the shield of faith with which you will be able to quench all the fiery darts of the wicked one. And take the helmet of salvation, and the sword of the Spirit, which is the word of God; praying always with all prayer and supplication in the Spirit." (Ephesians 6:11, 14-17)

"On this rock I will build My church, and the gates of Hades shall not prevail against it." (Matthew 16:18)

I AM noble and called according to Yahweh's purpose.

> "And we know that all things work together for good to those who love God, to those who are the called according to His purpose." (Romans 8:28)

> "But the ones that fell on the good ground are those who, having heard the word with a noble and good heart, keep it and bear fruit with patience." (Luke 8:15)

I AM a defender of the Gospel and full of His power.

> "But none of these things move me; nor do I count my life dear to myself, so that I may finish my race with joy, and the ministry which I received from the Lord Jesus, to testify to the gospel of the grace of God." (Acts 20:24)

> "For I am not ashamed of the gospel of Christ, for it is the power of God to salvation for everyone who believes, for the Jew first and also for the Greek." (Romans 1:16)

I AM able to trample on the serpent, the scorpion, the cobra and the lion and nothing shall harm me.

> "You shall tread upon the lion and the cobra, The young lion and the serpent you shall trample underfoot." (Psalm 91:13)

> "Behold, I give you the authority to trample on serpents and scorpions, and over all the power of the enemy, and nothing shall by any means hurt you." (Luke 10:19)

I AM confident that whatever I ask according to Yahweh's will, He will give it to me.

> "So I say to you, ask, and it will be given to you; seek, and you will find; knock, and it will be opened to you. For everyone who asks receives, and he who seeks finds, and to him who knocks it will be opened." (Luke 11:9-10)

I AM transformed and renewed by reading and listening to scriptures which were divinely given to mankind.

> "And do not be conformed to this world, but be transformed by the renewing of your mind, that you may prove what is that good and acceptable and perfect will of God." (Romans 12:2)

> "All Scripture is given by inspiration of God, and is profitable for doctrine, for reproof, for correction, for instruction in righteousness, that the man of God may be complete, thoroughly equipped for every good work." (2 Timothy 3:16)

I AM very blessed to give to others and impart all that Yahweh has given me.

> "And remember the words of the Lord Jesus, that He said, 'It is more blessed to give than to receive." (Acts 20:35)

I AM a sower of spiritual gifts and impartations by laying my hands on people and this will reap blessings in my everlasting and eternal life.

> "Therefore I remind you to stir up the gift of God which is in you through the laying on of my hands." (2 Timothy 1:6)

"Do not be deceived, God is not mocked; for whatever a man sows, that he will also reap. For he who sows to his flesh will of the flesh reap corruption, but he who sows to the Spirit will of the Spirit reap everlasting life." (Galatians 6:7-8)

I AM filled with Yahweh's knowledge, wisdom and understanding to fulfill His purpose on this earth.

"For this reason we also, since the day we heard it, do not cease to pray for you, and to ask that you may be filled with the knowledge of His will in all wisdom and spiritual understanding; that you may walk worthy of the Lord, fully pleasing Him, being fruitful in every good work and increasing in the knowledge of God." (Colossians 1:9-10)

I AM a doer of Yahweh's word because faith without works is dead.

"But be doers of the word, and not hearers only, deceiving yourselves." (James 1:22)

"Thus also faith by itself, if it does not have works, is dead. You see then that a man is justified by works, and not by faith only." (James 2:17, 24)

I AM full of Yahweh's joy, love and peace and I am more than a conqueror.

"But the fruit of the Spirit is love, joy, peace, longsuffering, kindness, goodness, faithfulness, gentleness, self-control." (Galatians 5:22-23)

"Yet in all these things we are more than conquerors

through Him who loved us." (Romans 8:37)

I AM chosen to proclaim praises to Yahweh and Yahshua through the word of my testimony.

> "But you are a chosen generation, a royal priesthood, a holy nation, His own special people, that you may proclaim the praises of Him who called you out of darkness into His marvelous light." (1 Peter 2:9)

> "And they overcame him by the blood of the Lamb and by the word of their testimony." (Revelation 12:11)

I AM heaven bound because I have an intimate relationship with Yahshua. Heaven is my home forever because earth is just my temporary home.

> "For we know that if our earthly house, this tent, is destroyed, we have a building from God, a house not made with hands, eternal in the heavens. For in this we groan, earnestly desiring to be clothed with our habitation which is from heaven." (2 Corinthians 5:1-2)

The Spirit of Yahweh causes these scriptures to come alive in our spirits so they can transform us and give us peace. His Word is power. He is Light. The Spirit of Yahweh says, *"Come and drink of the fountain of life. I am the fountain of life."*

> "For with You is the fountain of life;
> In Your light we see light." (Psalm 36:9)

~ CHAPTER TWO ~

The Spirit of Wisdom

The Spirit of Wisdom enables one to apply knowledge to life situations using biblical truths and by viewing wisdom through the perspective of Yahweh. Wisdom is like putting on a pair of reading glasses. Without the glasses, the words are blurry and unreadable, but with glasses, the words are clear and have meaning. Worldly wisdom has blurry lines that shift and change because there are no absolutes. Things shift depending on what makes you feel good for the day, the week, or the year. This is evident when people change jobs frequently because their career choice does not fulfill them. Instead of asking Papa Yahweh if they should take a particular job or follow a specific career, they choose without ever asking Him. Since He is the One who created you and He gifted you with certain abilities, He already sees your life from beginning to end. I do believe He qualifies to instruct you on your career or life path.

Worldly wisdom makes decisions based on profits, what makes you look or feel good, or how people will perceive you. Wisdom from on high makes decisions based on Yahweh's viewpoint. It is possible to know Yahweh's perspective when you actively seek His Spirit of Wisdom. The best place to acquire His wisdom is spending quite time with Him and choosing to apply biblical truths to your life. It isn't enough to have an impartation of His Spirit of Wisdom; you must actively seek His answers for your life. "If any of you lacks wisdom, let him ask of God, who gives to all liberally and without reproach, and it will be given to him" (James1:5).

When Moses led the Israelites out of Egypt, they had been slave laborers for years. Slavery had suppressed their creative abilities and shrouded their identity as Yahweh's chosen people. This was a rag tag bunch that hurriedly left Egypt with the spoils and riches of the ones who had enslaved them. When Papa Yahweh delivered them, He did it with pizazz and splendor. While they were in the wilderness, Yahweh gave Moses specific instructions to construct a tabernacle so His glorious presence would always be with them. They were well equipped to construct the tabernacle with the gold, silver, gems and material from the spoils of Egypt. The only thing they lacked was the skilled labor. But Yahweh was about to bring His tabernacle to the nation of Israel through His Spirit of Wisdom, Spirit of Knowledge, and Spirit of Understanding.

> "And Moses said to the children of Israel, "See, the Lord has called by name Bezalel the son of Uri, the son of Hur, of the tribe of Judah; and He has filled him with the Spirit of God, in wisdom and understanding, in knowledge and all manner of workmanship, to design artistic works, to work in gold and silver and bronze, in cutting jewels for setting, in carving wood, and to work in all manner of artistic workmanship." (Exodus 35:30-33)

The Lord imparted skills to Bezalel so he could be creative

and He wants to do the same for His people today. I sense deep in my spirit that there are several inventions that Yahweh wants to supernaturally impart to His children through His Spirit of wisdom, understanding, and knowledge. He is looking for someone who is willing to take the profits from these multi-million dollar inventions and use it for His glory in these last days. Just as He filled the people of Israel with His Spirit of wisdom, understanding, and knowledge to build the tabernacle, Yahweh will also fill His people to complete these innovations. Like I said before, we are living in exciting times. This is a season where there is going to be a great transfer of wealth to those whose hearts are set upon fulfilling Papa's kingdom plans.

It is biblical to transfer the Spirit of Wisdom through laying on of hands. Moses had died and the people were mourning the loss of his leadership. At the end of thirty days of weeping, the hearts of the people were encouraged when they realized that Joshua possessed the same Spirit of Wisdom as Moses. "Now Joshua the son of Nun was full of the spirit of wisdom, for Moses had laid his hands on him; so the children of Israel heeded him, and did as the Lord had commanded Moses" (Deuteronomy 34:9). Moses knew how imperative it was to have wisdom to execute the plans of Yahweh, that he imparted the Spirit of Wisdom to Joshua. True godly wisdom is having Yahweh's solution for every situation that arises in our lives and this can only happen through the Spirit of Wisdom.

Wisdom is an indispensable attribute of Yahweh which we all need to be successful in life. The Queen of Sheba understood the connection between wisdom and prosperity when she spoke these words to Solomon. "However I did not believe the words until I came and saw with my own eyes; and indeed the half was not told me. Your wisdom and prosperity exceed the fame of which I heard" (1 Kings 10:7). Wisdom and prosperity go hand in hand. When you have the Spirit of wisdom and begin to make wise decisions, then you will prosper in all areas of your life. The key to prospering is making conscious decisions to do what is right and moral in every situation, even when it is easier to cut corners. It is wisdom to pay all your taxes, even when you are paid in cash and there is no record. You think you are getting over on the government, but "Yahweh knows deceitful men; He sees wickedness also" (Proverbs 11:11). Wisdom says there are consequences to your actions and there is a principle of sowing and reaping. You cannot expect a holy God to bless and prosper lies and deceit. That would be contrary to His Word and character. By walking in wisdom, you position yourself to be blessed by Yahweh.

Wisdom asks questions like these and searches for the answers.
~ What are the ways of Yahweh?
~ What is something I do not know about Yahweh?
~ How does Yahweh want me to respond to this situation?
~ What are Yahweh's thoughts?

By asking questions like these and seeking the answers, we begin to have a deeper understanding of who He is. I am constantly asking my Papa questions. I have kept a spiritual journal for the last eighteen years and they contain countless questions to Yahweh. One morning I quickly wrote twelve questions to Papa in rapid succession. At the end of my labors I drew in a deep breath, knowing I had hurriedly written the questions without giving Papa a chance to answer. While I inspected my handiwork in my journal, Papa sweetly chided, *"Child, you are a woman of many questions."*

Then He patiently and systematically answered every question I posed to Him! Every answer came through His Spirit of Wisdom to my spirit and some of the answers astounded me!

While I was worshipping and honoring Yahweh and Yahshua on the Sabbath, I asked Papa Yahweh to reveal one thing about Himself that I did not know. It was my desire to know Him more intimately so I could be closer to Him. As soon as I asked the question, I got a vision of these beautiful diamonds floating in the air beside Yahweh's throne. Then Yahweh spoke these words to me. *"I think diamonds and they are."* I was amazed! Papa's thoughts create. I knew that His words create, but I did not realize that His thoughts create. Because I am made in His image, my thoughts can also create. It made me realize how important my thoughts truly are. It is so crucial to make sure all my thoughts are held captive through Christ because our minds are the greatest battlefield of Satan and his minions.

Sometimes in the middle of the night, my husband and I will wake at the same time and we pray together in tongues. One night the Spirit of Wisdom filled my husband and gave him this revelation about our thoughts. *"We travel at the speed of thought in the third heaven. The speed of thought makes the speed of light look like snail travel because the speed of thought is instant. When we go into the Holy of Holies through prayer and worship, we travel there at the speed of thought. At the moment we have the thought about being before Yahweh's throne, we are there! We think and it is. As the words form in our minds, it is. This is the speed of thought."* This is how I traveled in the spirit to heaven and hell in my book, "Heaven or Hell… Your Choice." I was in prayer and worship and at the speed of thought I was there in the spirit viewing the atrocities of hell and the beauty of heaven. In the earthly realm, we speak as fast as our thoughts come to us, so we need to weigh our words carefully. We will give an account for every idle word that tears people down instead of building them up.

In the third heaven, angels and heavenly hosts travel at the speed of thought and it is possible for us to travel from earth to the third heaven at the speed of thought. When we are in the spirit on earth through worship and prayer, we can travel at the speed of thought into the Holy of Holies in the third heaven. Going into the Holy of Holies through worship is a spiritual discipline. Worshipping Yahweh for only twenty minutes a week at a Sunday service is not sufficient to ascend into the Holy of Holies. You need to be a worshipper every day. Worship songs that ask Holy Spirit to come down or rain down is incorrect. Yahweh's Spirit does not come down. When we worship in spirit and truth, we rise up to His throne at the speed of thought. For this reason, our thoughts must be kept pure and holy at all times.

> "For though we walk in the flesh, we do not war according to the flesh. For the weapons of our warfare are not carnal but mighty in God for pulling down strongholds, casting down arguments and every high thing that exalts itself against the knowledge of God, bringing every thought into captivity to the obedience of Christ." (2 Corinthians 10:3-5)

Our thoughts must be dominated by the Spirit of Wisdom and wisdom says that worship is important. Holy Spirit showed me another dimension of worship that opened up my spiritual eyes. Yahshua instructed me to go to the 30th chapter of Exodus to unfold this awesome truth.

"And you shall anoint Aaron and his sons, and you shall consecrate them to minister as priests to Me." (Exodus 30:30 Hebraic Roots Bible)

Then Yahshua spoke these moving words to me. *"My child, you are consecrated to minister as a priest to Me, you are not a priest for Me."* I asked Yahshua how I was a priest to Him and He quickly responded, *"You are a priest to Me when you worship from the depths of your heart as you sing, dance, march, blow the shofar, and kneel down before Me. When you worship Me, you minister to Me. Now you can see why worship is so important! Your worship ministers to Me!"* I was so amazed that my worship ministered to Yahshua and this piece of wisdom has changed the depth of my worship.

We need to have appointments set aside to worship Yahshua and Yahweh. Unfortunately, some church services have become a microwave meal where the worship is a three song set which has little nutritional value for our spirit man. It tastes good, but does not sustain. It tickles our ears and entertains us, but has little transformational power. We must realize from the depths of our soul that we are created to worship Yahshua and Yahweh. Everything else in life is secondary. Everything! Our spouses, children, jobs, careers, vacations, hobbies, homes, and even ministry should be secondary to worshipping and loving Him.

Have you ever been to a prayer meeting or worship service and the words of the song are, "We want Your glory Lord. Send down Your Gory." We get so caught up with crying out for His glory because it makes us feel good. Here is a news flash. Yahweh doesn't always want us to feel good. Sometimes He desires us to be in repentance, weeping, and asking for forgiveness. I have been guilty of longing for His manifest glory just to appease my senses. We are spirit beings with a body and soul and it is the soul that longs for the manifest presence of Yahweh. Our spirits are already in communion with His glory and light. Yahshua spoke these words of wisdom to me which transformed my knowledge about the glory of the Yahweh.

"You say, "Show me Your glory." But I say, "You have My glory in you. You must display My glory to the nations. Worship Me and they will see My glory. Testify about Me and they will know My glory. Reach out and touch people and they will feel My glory. Take My glory into the nations. Wherever you go, I go. You will stand before kings and leaders of countries and display My glory."

Along with words of wisdom directly from the throne room, meditating on scriptures is a remarkable way to obtain wisdom. Sometimes we read bible passages and then put a big star on our forehead for doing our spiritual duty. The words only penetrate our minds, but they never permeate our spirits. The Word works when it saturates our spirits and this happens when we meditate on scripture. Obtaining wisdom means saturating your spirit with the Word and this can be accomplished by listening to an audio bible throughout the night as you sleep. The spoken Word infuses into your spirit and can perform miraculous things.

My husband is living proof that playing an audio Bible in the home releases miracles. In 1968, there were race riots in Washington, D.C. My husband was attacked by a group of black men and they caved his skull in with a thick green coke bottle. The doctors did their best to repair the damage to his smashed skull, but the bones did not mend evenly which left a hollow spot in his head along with a big scar. Many years later, Will began to play the audio bible in his bedroom 24 hours a day. After listening to the audio Bible for a couple of months, something supernatural happened. Will and his good friend were driving down the highway and Will began to rub his head with his hand. Suddenly he realized the hole in his head and the ragged bones were gone. He began to swerve on the highway because he was so shocked. When he examined his head in the mirror, the hole was gone, the ragged edge of the skull was smooth, and the scar vanished! Listening to the audio Bible released the Word into Will's spirit which in turn released a miracle.

This is another testimony to the wisdom of listening to an audio Bible. There was a young woman who was a new believer in Yahshua and she was married to an abusive alcoholic. Will sent her an audio Bible and she discretely placed it in her basement and played in on low so her husband could not detect it. Within three weeks, he gave his life to Christ which dramatically changed their marriage. By soaking her home in the Word of Yahweh, the spiritual atmosphere changed and the enemy went packing. There is wisdom in the Word. There is power in the Word. Yahshua is the Word and He came and dwelt among us.

Wisdom is releasing the Word and meditating on it. Meditate on these words of Solomon and embrace the value of wisdom.

"My son, if you receive my words,
And treasure my commands within you,
So that you incline your ear to wisdom,
And apply your heart to understanding;
Yes, if you cry out for discernment,
And lift up your voice for understanding,
If you seek her as silver,
And search for her as for hidden treasures;

Then you will understand the fear of the Lord,

And find the knowledge of God.

For the Lord gives wisdom;

From His mouth come knowledge and understanding;

He stores up sound wisdom for the upright;

He is a shield to those who walk uprightly;

He guards the paths of justice,

And preserves the way of His saints.

Then you will understand righteousness and justice,

Equity and every good path.

When wisdom enters your heart,

And knowledge is pleasant to your soul,

Discretion will preserve you;

Understanding will keep you,

To deliver you from the way of evil." (Proverbs 2:1-12)

~ CHAPTER THREE ~

The Spirit of Understanding

The Spirit of Understanding provides one with the supernatural ability to understand and discern the signs of the times and determine the outcome of events in advance. Belshazzar, the king of Babylon threw a big palace party and wanted to impress his lords and ladies. He commanded that all the gold vessels which were stolen from the temple in Jerusalem to be brought to the gala. While the revelers got drunk using these sacred cups, they praised the gods of gold and silver, bronze and iron, wood and stone. Yahweh's anger was stirred because of their contempt for Him, so He sent an undeniable message to the king. A floating hand appeared and wrote a message on the palace wall in full view of the king. The king became very nervous, so he called all the wise men of the land to give the interpretation. No one could give the interpretation which changed the entire atmosphere of the party. When the queen mother got wind of the situation, she scurried to the palace to bail out her son. She told the king about Daniel and how he had interpreted dreams for Nebuchadnezzar. Belshazzar summoned Daniel and he said to Daniel, "I have heard of you, that the Spirit of God is in you, and that light and understanding and excellent wisdom are found in you" (Daniel 5:14). Daniel interpreted the writing and told the king that because he had not humbled his heart, Yahweh was stripping him of his kingdom and dividing it between the Medes and the Persians. That same night, Belshazzar was killed and Darius the Mede received his kingdom.

Daniel was a man full of the Spirit of Understanding so he could decipher the message from Yahweh and proclaim the outcome before it happened. The gift of prophecy and words of knowledge operate hand in hand with the Spirit of Understanding. One can discern what is happening in the world and be aware of the signs of the times. Yahshua accused the Sadducees and the Pharisees of being dull of spirit because they could not discern that He was sent by Yahweh. They demanded that Yahshua show them a sign from heaven to verify that He was truly the Messiah. Yahshua admonished them sharply saying, "Hypocrites! You know how to discern the face of the sky, but you cannot discern the signs of the times" (Matthew 16:3). Yahshua was the Messiah sent by His Father and many scriptures pointed to this fact, and yet they had no spiritual understanding. They knew the Book of Isaiah and yet they could not connect this scripture to Yahshua because they did not have the Spirit of Understanding.

> "You are My witnesses," says the Lord,
> "And My servant whom I have chosen,
> That you may know and believe Me,
> And understand that I am He.
> Before Me there was no God formed,
> Nor shall there be after Me.
> I, even I, am the Lord,
> And besides Me there is no savior." (Isaiah 43:10-11)

We are His witnesses on this earth and we must have the Spirit of Understanding to discern global events, meteorological signs and earthly happenings. There is a great stirring and Holy Spirit is sending signs and messages in the heavens and on the earth. Those who desire to have understanding will receive His Spirit of Understanding, but those who want to keep their heads buried in the sand will not. Holy Spirit has given His warnings and messages to people who are seeking Him in spirit and truth. These are some prophetic dreams and visions, signs and messages that were given to me.

In this dream I saw a huge tanker ship being pulled by a tug boat because it was sinking from the weight it was carrying. The tanker ship was sinking in the back end and the front end was bobbing out of the water. In the dream the ship was called the "whale head" because only the front end was above the surface of the water and it looked like the head of a whale. Aboard were Japanese sailors wearing sea goggles to prevent the sea water from splashing in their eyes. The tanker was carrying waste by-products to be used by Japan, but became disabled. The ship was bottoming out as it was being towed toward Japan and I kept hearing this message over and over again: "Osaka Japan will be hit." Then I saw an oily sludge being washed on shore which destroyed an entire coastline and beach. At the end of the dream, this message was given to me by Holy Spirit. There will be four major events which will occur in one year.

Oil and sludge will destroy a coastline
Osaka Japan will be destroyed.
Great fires will erupt and destroy cities.
Mighty waters will destroy coastal areas.

These next two dreams and vision occurred within ten days of each other and they pertain to the United States. In this dream my husband and I were traveling in a vehicle in North Carolina. We were driving up a mountain road when we saw a policeman with his blue light flashing as a warning signal. He had stopped traffic which prevented us from proceeding up the mountain. In the dream, I got out of the vehicle and walked up the steep mountain road and the officer motioned for me to stop. Then all of a sudden a large wave rolled over the crest of the mountain and was heading towards me. I placed my back to the wave and was able to ride on the crest of it until it washed me back to the bottom of the mountain. At that moment in the dream, I knew that the Atlantic Ocean had washed in as far as this mountain in North Carolina.

In this second dream which occurred ten days later, I was at a beach on the East coast. There were many people at the beach enjoying the sand, sun and the ocean. There were some college aged boys who carried a couch and a rug to the edge of the shoreline as a joke. I warned them that the tide would come in and wash their couch away but they just ignored me and laughed. Then all of a sudden I saw this massive wave that was taller than the hotels and buildings and it was posed to crash onto the beach. In all my life, I had never seen a wave this high at the beach or in pictures. It towered above the tops of buildings.

The third warning about this massive wave came in a vision. In the vision, I was walking side by side with Yahshua in heaven and He spoke these words to me. *"Patricia, I want to show you some things."* Yahshua parted the clouds so I could see on the earth below. I saw myself on the earth and there was a mighty wave rising up ready to crash on the shore line. Before this mighty wave hit, I was lifted up. The wave was hundreds of feet tall. Then

Yahshua spoke these words to me.

"This wave will hit the East coast. Warn the people to get out. This mighty wave will devastate coastal cities and will wash inland for many miles. Florida will be decimated. Washington, D.C. will be under water. New York Harbor will flood the city. In North Carolina, the water will come as far as the mountains. The water will not go beyond the Appalachian Mountains. There are those who will not believe what you are reporting. They will perish in the wave. Millions of people will lose their lives. Nothing of this magnitude happens on the earth unless I speak it through My prophets. I have shown many of My prophets this tsunami and they are also reporting it will happen."

Yahshua did not give me a day or even a year when this massive tsunami wave will hit, He just instructed me to warn people. As a prophet of the Lord Most High, I am posting this warning for all to see. Many will think it could never happen and they will not heed this warning. But those who have an ear to hear what the Spirit of Understanding has revealed will take the necessary action to be safe. Ask Yahweh to give you His answer through His Seven Spirits.

Another area in which we need the Spirit of Understanding is the signs in our solar system. Yahweh created the sun, the moon, and the stars for signs as well to separate the seasons, days, and years. "Then God said, "Let there be lights in the firmament of the heavens to divide the day from the night; and let them be for signs and seasons, and for days and years" (Genesis 1:14). One of the signs of the moon is called a blood moon and there will be four blood moons that coincide with the Feasts of Israel. A blood moon is a total lunar eclipse with no partial lunar eclipses in between. There will be a tetrad or four successive blood moons that coincide with the Feasts of Passover and Sukkot in 2014 and 2015.

1st Blood Moon - April 15, 2014 Passover

2nd Blood Moon - October 8, 2014 Sukkot

3rd Blood Moon - April 4, 2015 Passover

4th Blood Moon - September 28, 2015 Sukkot

In the last 500 years, there have been only two tetrads that have come on the Feast days of Israel. One tetrad occurred in 1949-1950 which was one year after Israel made the announcement they were an independent nation. On May 14, 1948, Israel made a declaration that they were a nation and immediately several Arab nations waged a war against them. In 1949, Israel won the War of Independence and signed peace agreements with these Arab nations. The second tetrad occurred in 1967-1968 about six weeks before the Six Day War of 1967. Israel won this war also. Every time there has been a tetrad of blood moons on Yahweh's feast days, there has been a war with Israel and Israel has won the war. The next tetrad is coming in 2014 and 2015. Will there be another war involving Israel? Will Israel regain more territory or possibly build the 3rd temple? The Spirit of Understanding has opened our eyes to be aware of these events.

Another year that needs to be closely examined regarding Israel and those who love Yahshua the Messiah is 2017. The year 2017 is the 50th anniversary of Israel retaking Jerusalem during the Six Day War of 1967, the 50th anniversary of the discovery of the Dead Sea Scrolls, and the 500th anniversary of the Protestant movement which occurred in 1517. In 1517 is also when the Turks conquered Jerusalem and took possession of it from the Mamluk Dynasty. This is important because Rabbi Judah Ben Samuel wrote a prophecy 300 years before the Turks conquered Jerusalem. This is his amazing prophecy which has proven accurate.

"When the Ottomans (Turks) conquer Jerusalem they will rule over Jerusalem for eight jubilees. Afterwards Jerusalem will become no-man's land for one jubilee, and then in the ninth jubilee it will once again come back into the possession of the Jewish nation – which would signify the beginning of the Messianic end time." [1]

A jubilee is 50 years according to scriptures and eight jubilees would be 400 years. We know by history that the Ottoman Turks gained control of Jerusalem in the year 1517 and held power over Jerusalem for 400 years. They were conquered by the British military forces under the command of British military General Edmund Allenby on December 17, 1917. The British Mandate gave the land of Israel and Jerusalem over to the control of the British.

Then the prophecy continues when it states; "Afterwards Jerusalem will become no-man's land for one jubilee." It is amazing that from 1917 when the British Mandate controlled the city of Jerusalem, Jerusalem became under international law a "no-man's land for one jubilee". Fifty years later, the Israeli army captured the city of Jerusalem in the Six Day War on June 17, 1967. Exactly in one jubilee, the control and ownership of Jerusalem was returned to the Jewish-Israelis. This was the first time the Israelis gained control of Jerusalem since the day it was destroyed in AD 70.

There is one jubilee or 50 years remaining in Judah Ben Samuel's prophecy. When the final jubilee is added to 1967, it brings us to the year 2017. Rabbi Judah Ben Samuel predicted there would be 10 Jubilees once the gentiles took Jerusalem. At the end of 500

1 http://destination-yisrael.biblesearchers.com/destination-yisrael/2012/12/rabbi-judah-ben-samuels-jubilee-prophecy-gives-the-year-of-the-messiah.html#sthash.s7KTsBcH.dpuf

years, the "Messianic end time" would begin and that is the year 2017! When he was asked where he received his wisdom from, his answer was: "The prophet Elijah, who will precede the Messiah, appeared to me and revealed many things to me and emphasized that the precondition for answered prayer is that it is fueled by enthusiasm and joy for the greatness and holiness of God."

What does Judah Ben Samuel prophecy imply when he stated it would be the beginning of Messianic end times? Will the beginning of Messianic end times be when the Israelis embrace Yahshua as their Messiah? Currently, only 1% of Israeli Jews believe that Yahshua is the Messiah. Will this be the beginning of getting ready for the return of Yahshua our Messiah? Will 2017 be the year that a peace treaty is signed with Israel which will mark the beginning of the seven year tribulation? We are living in exciting times and one cannot ignore Judah Ben Samuel's prophecy or the tetrad of blood moons. More than ever, we need the Spirit of Understanding.

The disciples asked Yahshua what the signs of the times which would indicate the end of the age. In Luke 21, Yahshua gave his disciples a very specific sequence of events that would happen before the end of the age would occur. He told His disciples that Jerusalem would be surrounded by armies and many would die by the sword and be led away captive into all the nations. This happened in AD 70 when the Romans burned Jerusalem, destroyed the temple, slaughtered many Jews, and many were exiled into the nations. Next Yahshua said, "And Jerusalem will be trampled by Gentiles until the times of the Gentiles are fulfilled" (Luke 21:24). Jerusalem remained under the control of the Gentiles from AD 70 until 1967 when Israel regained ownership. Jerusalem was indeed trampled by the Gentiles for a season and the end of that period was fulfilled in 1967. Next Yahshua said this, "And there will be signs in the sun, in the moon, and in the stars; and on the earth distress of nations, with perplexity, the sea and the waves roaring; men's hearts failing them from fear and the expectation of those things which are coming on the earth, for the powers of the heavens will be shaken" (Luke 21:25-26). We are currently in this portion of the prophetic sequence where there are signs in the heavens and the waves are roaring. We have witnessed massive tsunamis in the Indian Ocean in 2004 and the tsunami that hit Japan in 2011. I believe the East coast tsunami I saw in the dreams will surpass in magnitude both of these previous tsunamis. There will be other signs yet to come as stars fall to the earth, the sun is darkened, mountains are flattened, and islands disappear in the ocean. "Then they will see the Son of Man coming in a cloud with power and great glory. Now when these things begin to happen, look up and lift up your heads, because your redemption draws near" (Luke 21:27-28).

John was given a vivid description of these same events that Yahshua spoke about to His disciples and he described them in the book of Revelation. When all these prophecies are pieced together through the Spirit of Understanding, one cannot help but realize that we are rapidly heading towards the Messianic end times.

> "I looked when He opened the sixth seal, and behold, there was a great earthquake; and the sun became black as sackcloth of hair, and the moon became like blood. And the stars of heaven fell to the earth, as a fig tree drops its late figs when it is shaken by a mighty wind. Then the sky receded as a scroll when it is rolled up, and every mountain and island was moved out of its place. And the kings of the earth, the great men, the rich men, the commanders, the

mighty men, every slave and every free man, hid themselves in the caves and in the rocks of the mountains, and said to the mountains and rocks, "Fall on us and hide us from the face of Him who sits on the throne and from the wrath of the Lamb! For the great day of His wrath has come, and who is able to stand?" (Revelation 6:12-17)

CHAPTER FOUR

The Spirit of Counsel

"*My child, I know all things. I know the beginning and I know the end of all things. It is wisdom to seek My counsel regarding your life. It is wisdom to seek My advice in all decisions. The more you ask My advice in all decisions, the easier your life will become. Many people make decisions based on their emotions and their soul instead of asking Me. When they get into trouble, they quickly ask Me to bail them out. If they invoked My Spirit of Counsel first, they would not get into trouble.*"

In these last days it is imperative that we consult the Spirit of Counsel because there will be countless lies and deception that could confuse us. Outward circumstances may appear to be one thing, but the reality of the situation can be been hidden through fraud and deceit. This happened to the Israelites when they began their conquests in the Promised Land. They had been instructed through Moses to take possession of all the land and to kill all the inhabitants of the land. The Israelites had already conquered Jericho and Ai and were zealous to conquer more nations. The inhabitants of Gibeon sent ambassadors to Joshua to sign a peace agreement under the pretext they were from a faraway land. The men of Gibeon dressed in tattered clothing, worn out sandals, and carried moldy bread and old wine skins to facilitate their deception. Joshua made a covenant of peace with the Gibeonites based on their false testimony and their outward appearance, instead of seeking the counsel of the Lord.

> "Then the men of Israel took some of their provisions; but they did not ask counsel of the Lord. So Joshua made peace with them, and made a covenant with them to let them live; and the rulers of the congregation swore to them. And it happened at the end of three days, after they had made a covenant with them that they heard that they were their neighbors who dwelt near them." (Joshua 9:14-16)

There are consequences to making agreements with people without first seeking Yahweh's Spirit of Counsel. How many Christian men and women make agreements in business or their personal life without first seeking Yahweh and then suffer the consequences? As a result of the peace covenant with the Gibeonites, Israel suffered a three year famine. When David inquired of the Lord the reason for the famine, His answer was this: "It is because of Saul and his bloodthirsty house, because he killed the Gibeonites" (2 Samuel 21:1). Yahweh punished Israel with a famine for breaking the peace agreement with the Gibeonites, even many years later. It did not matter that the Israelites were duped into the covenant; they were still bound by it. Once we make an agreement with a person, we must keep our word. It is important to seek Yahweh regarding all our decisions that will have future consequences, so we are not bound by ill-advised choices.

"Woe to the rebellious children," says the Lord,
"Who take counsel, but not of Me,
And who devise plans, but not of My Spirit,
That they may add sin to sin;
Who walk to go down to Egypt,
And have not asked My advice." (Isaiah 30:1-2)

"David My servant understood the importance of seeking My advice. Before he went into battle, he asked My counsel first. When I instructed him to go into battle, David knew he would have victory. When I told him not to go into battle, he remained neutral because he knew he would be defeated. Does it not make sense to ask Me for My advice when I know all things? There is nothing too small to ask Me. My ear is bent towards those who seek My counsel. You, My child, are one of those who seek My counsel and you have My ear. I hear your words. I hear your prayers. I hear your cries. I hear your songs of worship. My ear is bent towards you."

Papa Yahweh hears our prayers. He knows our requests even before we speak the words. There have been times when I have thought a prayer in my mind, and before I spoke the prayer, Papa answered me. At those times, I absolutely know that I am hearing His counsel. His heartbeat is my heartbeat. The Spirit of Counsel is eagerly waiting to saturate us with advice, guidance, direction, and warning. But first we must seek Him and ask questions like these.

~ Yahweh, what is Your advice regarding this situation?
~ Yahweh, should I go to this place?
~ Yahweh, are there people in my inner circle You want to remove or add?
~ Yahweh, what is my destiny according to Your plans?

Papa's eyes are scanning to and fro throughout the earth, searching for those who will call upon His counsel. When He finds one, He rejoices because He can openly reward that person for following His counsel.

"You are great in counsel and mighty in work, for Your eyes are open to all the ways of the sons of men, to give everyone according to his ways and according to the fruit of his doings." (Jeremiah 32:19)

The Spirit of Counsel also enables us to hear Yahweh's response so we can follow His direction. This is a message and vision from Yahweh which gives guidance to His children. *"Tell My people not to be like Lot's wife. Do not look back and lose your life, but press onward to the high calling of serving Yahweh."* Then in a vision I saw a set of stairs. There were people on every step of this stairway. The Spirit of Counsel showed me there are various levels of serving Yahweh. When we obey the Lord, we rise to the next level on the stairway. Unfortunately, many people were still at the first level of the stairs. I asked Yahshua how I could motivate people so they could move up the steps of serving Him. This was His response to me.

"Child, even I had those in My inner circle. I saw which ones were passionate and which ones who were standing by to observe the outcome of My earthly ministry. You cannot change the hearts of people to persuade them to serve Me. But you can teach those who are willing and impart the Seven Spirits to them. Your zeal will be evident to people and some will catch your fire. Others will observe you to see if the outcome of what you are professing is true. Many will see what you speak is truth and will believe."

Sometimes the Spirit of Counsel can visit in the middle of the night when our body is at rest and our mind is quieted. There are times when Holy Spirit wakes me between 1:00 AM and 3:00 AM and downloads messages to me. It usually begins with a few words repeated over and over again in my mind until I realize it is His Spirit speaking to me. I get up and write the phrase and then the Spirit of Counsel continues to download more revelation as I pray in the Spirit. I have received some powerful direction and warnings in these night watches. David, the Psalmist also knew what it was like to receive counsel from the Lord in the middle of the night.

"I will bless the Lord who has given me counsel;
My heart also instructs me in the night seasons.
I have set the Lord always before me;
Because He is at my right hand I shall
not be moved." (Psalm 16:7-8)

One instance I woke in the middle of the night and two Bible verses were given to me through Holy Spirit. These verses were being recited into my spirit so He could impart His counsel.

"It is the glory of God to conceal a matter, But the glory of kings is to search out a matter." (Proverbs 25:2)

"For I know the thoughts that I think toward you, says the Lord, thoughts of peace and not of evil, to give you a future and a hope. Then you will call upon Me and go and pray to Me, and I will listen to you. And you will seek Me and find Me, when you search for Me with all your heart." (Jeremiah 28:11-13)

I began to meditate on these scriptures and the common

theme that was imparted to my spirit was to "diligently search." Immediately I penned this prayer. "Papa, I am searching to know You more. I want to be intimately close to You, even more than I am at this moment. I want to be immersed in Your heart. I desire to know what truly brings You joy, laughter, and my love. I am Your lover who wants to know every detail about her Beloved. I was created by You in Your image. By discovering You, I truly discover me. Can You give me a word that will help me in my search to know You more intimately?" Immediately Papa answered, *"Psalm 33."* After reading Psalm 33, Holy Spirit quickened these verses in my spirit.

> "The counsel of Yahweh stands forever, the thoughts of His heart from generation to generation. Blessed is the nation whose Elohim is Yahweh, the people He has chosen for His inheritance." (Psalm 33:11-12 Hebraic Roots Bible)

By now, you can see I truly am a woman of many questions because I asked Papa Yahweh this question, "What are the thoughts of Your heart that go from generation to generation?" Papa answered, *"To have a people who love Me."* My heart was so touched by His answer that a tear ran down my cheek. Yahweh is love and He created us to reflect His love and nothing will thwart His plan to have a people who truly love Him. This was His plan when He created Adam and Eve and this was His plan when He sent His Son Yahshua to take the punishment for the sin of mankind.

Yahshua loves us and through His love and concern, He gave me this message to proclaim. *"My child, you are My watchman. Lift up your voice and proclaim that I am coming very very soon. My people are going about their lives without a sense of My imminent return. Prepare the way of the LORD. Make unto you paths of righteousness. Clear the way. Get ready. Forge ahead with the Gospel and many will get saved. They will see My salvation working through their bodies and souls.*"

You cannot have one foot in the world and one foot in Christianity and expect to see the salvation of Yahweh. With Yahweh, it is all or nothing. We are at a time when there is a line drawn in the sand and there is no in between. Which side are you on? An 84 year old prophetess spoke these words on her deathbed in 2014 and her prophecy also confirms that we need to choose a side. The Spirit of Counsel is warning us and preparing us for what is to come.

"Thus saith the Lord: "My beloved people. Very soon now you will see a 'happening' (an event) that only My people who are very close to Me will understand what they are seeing. Are you awake? Are you listening for My voice? Are you completely and totally yielded to Me? Then don't fret …but be at peace with Me. My own must know Me and know My Word. Yes, I do tell you that very often for it is essential for your walk with Me. I am Your all in all. In your nation, which is totally against Me, there are only those who are Mine or those who hate Me. Too many of you are trying to walk with one foot in either path, and those I consider to be in the enemy's camp. Remember! I never told you it would be easy. I must look at you and see that you are holding onto no one or nothing in this world, only to your Lord God Almighty."[2]

When the Spirit of Counsel penetrates your spirit, hold onto Him alone and seek His advice, direction, and guidance. The Spirit of Counsel has all the answers to the universe and He is the One I cling to. Contemplate the greatness of Yahweh through His Spirit of Counsel, just as Isaiah did.

---

2 Prophecy given by 84 year old Katie Jordan on her deathbed.

"Who has measured the waters in the hollow of His hand,
Measured heaven with a span
And calculated the dust of the earth in a measure?
Weighed the mountains in scales
And the hills in a balance?
Who has directed the Spirit of the Lord,
Or as His counselor has taught Him?
With whom did He take counsel, and who instructed Him,
And taught Him in the path of justice?
Who taught Him knowledge,
And showed Him the way of understanding?"
(Isaiah 40:12-14)

~ CHAPTER FIVE ~

The Spirit of Might

Who is the Spirit of Might and why have we not heard about the Seven Spirits of Yahweh, much less the Spirit of Might? Over the centuries why has religion tried to silence the truth? The plain and simple fact is that the enemy has used religion to dilute truth so he can render us powerless. Satan infiltrated the church with distorted doctrines which bred spiritual weakness. Spiritual weakness led to mediocrity which took some people down the path of heresy. A powerless Christian is not able to enforce the victory Yahshua already proclaimed over Satan, so we desperately need the Spirit of Might to strengthen us.

> "Have you not known?
> Have you not heard?
> The everlasting God, the Lord,
> The Creator of the ends of the earth,
> Neither faints nor is weary.
> His understanding is unsearchable.
> He gives power to the weak,
> And to those who have no might He increases strength." (Isaiah 40:28-29)

The Book of Judges is a fundamental model of how Satan's lies spiritually weakened the Israelites which led them into far-reaching heresy. The people of Israel lived with and interbred with foreigners, which was forbidden by Yahweh. After being spiritually weakened by the people of other nations, they would forsake Yahweh and worship their gods, Baal and Ashtoreth. When they practiced this evil, Yahweh would give Israel into the hands of their enemies who would plunder and destroy them. The Lord gave Israel into the hands of the Midianites for seven years because of their idol worship. The Midianites would invade the land of Israel and destroy their crops and kill all their animals, which left them impoverished.

Gideon was fearfully threshing his wheat in a winepress to keep it hidden from the Midianites when an Angel of the Lord appeared to him. The Angel made this peculiar proclamation in light of the circumstances he found Gideon. "The Lord is with you, you mighty man of valor! Go in this might of yours, and you shall save Israel from the hand of the Midianites. Have I not sent you?" (Judges 6:11,14). Immediately Gideon made excuses that he was from the weakest clan and he was the least in his father's house. In other words, he was a pathetic weakling with no backbone to fight. "And the Lord said to him, "Surely I will be with you, and you shall defeat the Midianites as one man" (Judges 6:16). The Spirit of Might strengthened Gideon and he did defeat the Midianites with ordinary men following extraordinary instructions from Yahweh. Three hundred men armed with only trumpets, empty pitchers, and torches, defeated the entire Midianite army! It is amazing what the Spirit of Might can accomplish.

Yahweh is calling some of His children who are ordinary people to accomplish spectacular feats by receiving the Spirit of

Might. These endeavors are much greater than what an average individual can accomplish. But with the Spirit of Might, all things are possible. Some may be called to feed hundreds of thousands of people, to be a safe house for Christians and Jews in perilous times, to spend days in continuous prayer, to establish healing centers, or to preach the gospel before millions. I remember years ago when the Lord called me to be His evangelist to the nations. I asked Him this question, "Why would you choose a small town housewife to do such great things for You?" This was my Gideon response to such a monumental undertaking, and yet He loving said this to me. *"I choose the weak things of this earth to confound the wise."* I was not aware at the time He placed His calling upon my life that He would empower me with His Seven Spirits to be His evangelist and His prophet. I can take no credit for all the wonderful works He has done through me. What I can say is that I love Him with all my heart, mind, soul, and strength. What I can say is when I am weak, He makes me strong.

In the natural realm, it does not make sense that weakness can bring about spiritual power. But it does. Fasting is a prime example of making the body weak to make the spirit strong. More often than not, we live through our emotions and our minds. We appease the demands of our body while preventing our spirit from being in control. When our body is denied food, our spirit becomes elevated above our soul and our body. As our body becomes weak through fasting, our spirit can take its rightful place. I know when I fast, I hear more clearly from Holy Spirit and I get more revelation. I also become more spiritually powerful. Fasts can be a tool to defeat the plans of the enemy in your life and in the lives of others. One great way to have victory over the enemy is through activating the Spirit of Might during a fast. Yahweh spoke these words through

Isaiah about the importance of fasting and it's correlation to having spiritual power over the works of the enemy.

"Is this not the fast that I have chosen:
To loose the bonds of wickedness,
To undo the heavy burdens,
To let the oppressed go free,
And that you break every yoke?
Is it not to share your bread with the hungry,
And that you bring to your house the poor
who are cast out;
When you see the naked, that you cover him,
And not hide yourself from your own flesh?"
(Isaiah 58:6-7)

Yahshua understood the power of fasting and how fasting activated spiritual power and might within Him. He had been baptized by John and filled with Holy Spirit and immediately he was led into the desert by Holy Spirit. Yahshua fasted for forty days and after at the end of forty days, He was tempted by Satan. His fast activated spiritual power within Him to withstand the temptations of Satan. It is interesting because scriptures states that Yahshua went into the wilderness, He was filled with Holy Spirit, but He returned in the power of Holy Spirit. "Then Jesus returned in the power of the Spirit to Galilee, and news of Him went out through all the surrounding region" (Luke 4:14). Fasting brings spiritual power. Fasting is preparation to accomplish enormous undertakings for Yahweh. Fasting allows the Spirit of Might to strengthen the spirit of man when the body is weak. "My grace is sufficient for you, for My strength is made perfect in weakness" (2 Corinthians 12:9).

Micah understood his strength in the Lord when he had

to confront the wicked rulers and the false prophets who were declaring peace where there was no peace. These evil leaders lulled the people into believing that all was well with Israel, even in the midst of bloodshed, iniquity, and injustice. The town councilmen were passing judgments for a bribe, the priests were preaching for profit, and the prophets were speculating for a fortune. Sadly enough, this sounds like the government and the religious system of America today. Micah warned the people about the impending judgment because of their covenant breaking disloyalty to Yahweh. It was through the power of the Spirit of Might, coupled with his heart for justice, that Micah spoke these words.

> "But truly I am full of power by the Spirit of the Lord,
> And of justice and might,
> To declare to Jacob his transgression
> And to Israel his sin." (Micah 3:8)

It was a tough assignment to openly declare the sins of his friends and neighbors, but that was what Micah did. I am sure his life had to be pure and holy, or the Israelites would have pointed an accusatory finger at him. Can you imagine if the Spirit of the Lord came upon a pastor and he began to announce the sins of individual people in his congregation? One of two things would happen. Either the person would fall to their knees in repentance, or they would leave the church in anger. Confronting sin is not an easy thing. Honestly confronting our own sin is something we all need to do. If sin is not dealt with, then we run the risk of being disciplined by our heavenly Father. Micah emphasized Yahweh's justice and love in disciplining the nation of Israel and also presented Him as the sovereign Lord of the earth who controls the destinies of the nations. The Spirit of Might enabled Micah to stand strong with the truth, even when his message was not widely accepted. As born again Christians, we need to stand firm and strong against what we know is wrong, even when the world labels us right winged fanatics. We desperately need the Spirit of Might to withstand the barrage of insults and the persecution. Ultimately we may need the supernatural ability to stare death in the face and not back down from His truth.

In the fifth seal of Revelation, there were martyrs positioned under an altar and they were crying out for their blood to be avenged.

> "Then a white robe was given to each of them; and it was said to them that they should rest a little while longer, until both the number of their fellow servants and their brethren, who would be killed as they were, was completed." (Revelation 6:11)

There are a set number of Yahweh's people who will be martyred before Yahshua raptures the believers. The world will vehemently come against the Christians and kill us because we stand for truth and righteousness. This is a difficult message that many people do not want to hear. But I refuse to be like the prophets who Micah admonished because they lulled the people into believing that all was well with the nation of Israel. All is not well with our nation. We are a nation of corruption, lies, deceit, and immorality, all of monumental proportion. Yahweh's hand of judgment will come because He is full of justice, but He will strengthen His children to endure with the Spirit of Might.

> "That He would grant you, according to the riches of His glory, to be strengthened with might through His Spirit in the inner man that Christ may dwell in yourhearts through faith." (Ephesians 3:16-17)

"The Spirit of Might strengthens people to win the battle in the spiritual realm. My child, battles are won in the spiritual realm first, before the victory is manifested in the natural realm. The Spirit of Might strengthens My people through prayer and intercession, it has little to do with physical strength. Although there could be times when My Spirit of Might strengthens a person for a physical battle, the physical strengthening only comes after the spiritual strengthening."

"The Spirit of Might is a spiritual strengthening to accomplish mighty works I have set forth for an individual. I have called My people to be a force of power against the works of the enemy. People are not your enemies. People can become your enemy when Satan uses them as his pawns. Remember, you do not wrestle against flesh and blood. You battle against principalities, powers, rulers of darkness, and wickedness in high places. The Spirit of Might enables you to battle the spiritual forces of darkness. Rise up and take your rightful place. I have placed the Sword of My Word in your hand. Wield your sword! The enemy cannot stand in the presence of My Word. Use My Word, it activates the Spirit of Might against Satan."

I had a spiritual encounter that displayed the Spirit of Might. I was in a spiritual battle that was meant to destroy me, or at the very least, incapacitate me. I was crying out to Papa and asking Him to show me how to do battle. I was reciting several scriptures every day for forty days when the battle intensified. I was praying in the Spirit and I sensed it was time to take action. Immediately my spirit was lifted into the second heaven and I saw a red dragon and several witches flying on brooms. I had heard stories that witches flew on brooms, but now I was actually seeing it in the spiritual realm. Then the Spirit of Might showed me a sword with a jewel encrusted handle. At first I was reluctant to take the sword in my hand, so the Spirit of Might told me to grasp my husband's hand. As soon as I clutched his hand, I knew I had my husband's spiritual covering and I suddenly became fearless. I valiantly swung the heavy sword over my head in a sweeping motion with the zeal of a warrior. The sword severed the head of the dragon and when he was decapitated, the witches fell out of the sky and plummeted to the earth.

There was much that I learned from this encounter. The first thing I learned was I released His Word by declaring scriptures out loud which activated the Spirit of Might. There is great power in praying scriptures because His Word is living and powerful and cannot return to Him empty. Second, I understood that this attack against me was in the spiritual realm which manifested in the natural realm. The Spirit of Might gave me His strength to battle an enemy in the second heaven which was a spiritual battle. Once the spiritual battle was won, I would have victory in the earthly realm. Third, I needed my husband to complete the mission because he is my spiritual covering and I have more power when we join together. "Five of you shall chase a hundred, and a hundred of you shall put ten thousand to flight; your enemies shall fall by the sword before you" (Leviticus 26:8). Fourth, I learned there is a hierarchy in the spiritual realm. When I took out the chief dragon through the Spirit of Might, the inferior ones lost their power. I witnessed this when the dragon's head was cut off and the witches fell to the ground. The witches derived their power and capability from the red dragon. Satan has been defeated by Yahshua and we are called to rise up and take our rightful place to enforce His victory. Satan does not want us to have the Spirit of Might because he knows the damage we can do to his kingdom. Now you can see why he has blinded the church with a watered down message that does not teach about the Seven Spirits of Yahweh. I have witnessed the Spirit of Might in action against my enemy in the second heaven.

> "Oh, that they were wise, that they understood this,
> That they would consider their latter end!
> How could one chase a thousand,
> And two put ten thousand to flight,
> Unless their Rock had sold them,
> And the Lord had surrendered them?
> For their rock is not like our Rock."
> (Deuteronomy 32:29-31)

I had a dream where the Spirit of Might was my powerful deliverer during a time of persecution. In this dream, my husband and I were at an airport. We were talking with a woman and I began to pray in tongues over her. Suddenly a burly police woman approached me and told me that praying with people was illegal. My husband ignored the outburst of the officer and he shielded me and began to pray in tongues also. The policewoman was ready to arrest us and I reached up and gently placed both my hands on her cheeks. She crumbled to the floor like a rag doll and when she tried to get up, she could not. Her body was pinned to the floor, much to her dismay. We ran to an escalator to get away and just as we were at the top of the escalator we could see the police woman stagger to her feet. The Spirit of Might kept her on the floor until we were safe. When I woke from this dream, Yahweh spoke these words to me. ***"The adversary was trying to prevent you and your husband from baptizing people with My Spirit. Know that when the opposition comes, I will provide a way so you can continue*** *to baptize people with My Spirit and fire."* The way that Yahweh provides is through His Spirit of Might.

~ CHAPTER SIX ~

The Spirit of Knowledge

The Spirit of Knowledge is not about acquiring cerebral knowledge. It is not an intellectual or analytical process by which we obtain more information. Yahweh described the Spirit of Knowledge in this way. ***"The Spirit of Knowledge enables one to see things as I see them. When knowledge is darkened through sin and the works of the enemy, truth cannot be grasped. Darkened knowledge means that people do and say things that are right in their own eyes. The Spirit of Knowledge opens the eyes of a person to see as I see. The eyes are the window to the soul and spirit. The Spirit of Knowledge transfers truth from the spirit to the mind and then an individual can choose to embrace the truth or reject it. My prophets have a Spirit of Knowledge. They are seers. They see things as I see things and then they announce what they have been shown."***

I found it very fascinating that Yahweh said the Spirit of Knowledge enables one to see things as He sees things. The Hebrew root word for knowledge is *"yada"* which means "to know, to ascertain by seeing." The Spirit of Knowledge allows us to see and learn spiritual truth so we can apply it to our lives. When knowledge is inaccurate, we sin against Yahweh. We live through the grid of our distorted acquired knowledge and act according to what we think is right. If we live this way long enough, sin becomes the cultural norm and we become numb to what Yahweh declares is right. Doesn't that sound familiar in our country where killing unborn babies is a mother's right, same sex marriages is touted as normal, and mind altering drugs are being legalized. There is a consequence to rejecting knowledge and refusing to see things the way Yahweh sees things.

> "My people are destroyed for lack of knowledge. Because you have rejected knowledge, I also will reject you from being priest for Me; Because you have forgotten the law of your God, I also will forget your children." (Hosea 4:6)

Jeremiah was a prophet and a seer and he operated under the Spirit of Knowledge. He was prophesying about the judgment of Yahweh that was coming to Jerusalem because they disobeyed Yahweh's voice and had forsaken His covenant. The Israelites set up altars in every street in Jerusalem and Judah to worship the foreign gods. The men of Anathoth were incensed that Jeremiah was prophesying the Lord's rebuke as a result of their sin, so they conspired to kill him. While the conspiracy against Jeremiah's life was being planned in secret, Yahweh warned Jeremiah. "Now the Lord gave me knowledge of it, and I know it; for You showed me their doings" (Jeremiah 11:18). The Spirit of Knowledge came upon Jeremiah and gave him a word of knowledge about the plot to take his life. In the days of the biblical prophets, the Spirits of Yahweh came upon the prophets, but did not remain on them. We have the blessing of living after Pentecost whereby the Spirits of Yahweh are with us continually. But with that beautiful blessing come accountability and responsibility.

"For the Lord is the God of knowledge;
And by Him actions are weighed." (1 Samuel 2:3)

The Spirit of Knowledge will warn us of events to come, just as He did for Jeremiah. As a body of believers in this time in history, we need the Spirit of Knowledge. We need words of knowledge from Yahweh to discern and understand these last days before Yahshua returns. The intensity with which I have been receiving messages through the Spirit of Knowledge has increased. There is a stirring in my spirit that time is very short and people need to be equipped and empowered quickly.

The prophets of old were seers and the prophets today are still seers. They see events and the condition of the hearts of the people the way Yahweh sees them. When the ancient prophets announced the messages of Yahweh, the people responded in a negative way. Isaiah spoke these words to rebellious Israel and his words are still relevant to defiant people today.

"That this is a rebellious people,
Lying children,
Children who will not hear the law of the Lord;
Who say to the seers, "Do not see,"
And to the prophets, "Do not prophesy to us right things;
Speak to us smooth things, prophesy deceits.
Get out of the way,
Turn aside from the path,
Cause the Holy One of Israel
To cease from before us." (Isaiah 30:9-11)

As a nation, we are much like the Israelites because we do

not want to hear about the Ten Commandments, much less follow them. A large portion of the church wants the feel good hallelujah messages that don't confront sin. Holiness and righteousness have become an antiquated ideal that has been replaced by the attitude that once I am saved I am in the kingdom. Arrogance says I can live the way I want to because grace covers all my sins. These are lies from the pit of hell to lull Yahweh's children into rebellion. The Spirit of Knowledge teaches us how to live.

"The Spirit of Knowledge unveils biblical principles and shows one the practical life application. This is much more than a mental ascent of scriptures. It is living My Word because My Spirit of Knowledge has quickened it. Words cannot be transformational without My Spirit of Knowledge. When you speak words through the Spirit of Knowledge, they release My power to accomplish what you speak. My Word will always accomplish the thing for which I sent it."

The Spirit of Knowledge takes the words of the Bible and makes them living and active in the life of a believer. The only way to receive the Seven Spirits of Yahweh is to be born anew through Yahshua. When we are born again by the power of Holy Spirit, our spirits are made perfect and we have Yahweh's righteousness, His holiness, His perfect health, His power, His wisdom, and His success all in Christ. This powerful truth can only come through the Spirit of Knowledge and it is quickened through the Spirit of Understanding.

When we are born again, we no longer are bound by the laws of nature; we are now under the Law of the Spirit. "The law of the Spirit of life in Christ Jesus has made me free from the law of sin and death" (Romans 8:2). The reason Yahshua could fearlessly reach out and touch the lepers without getting the disease was not because He was the Son of God. The reason Yahshua could come in contact with any contagious disease and not get sick was because He knew the Law of the Spirit made Him free from the laws of nature.

John G. Lake also knew this biblical truth. He was a healing evangelist of the early 1900's in South Africa. When the bubonic plague struck Africa, he fearlessly ministered to people who were infected with this deadly disease. He took the foam from the mouth of a person with the plague in his bare hands and placed his hand under a microscope. The plague died in his hands while doctors viewed it under the microscope. When the astounded doctors asked him why the disease died and he did not contract the plague, John G. Lake quoted Romans 8:2. He knew that he was no longer under the laws of nature, but under the Law of the Spirit he received in Christ.

The Spirit of Knowledge tells us that we possess the same Law of the Spirit that Yahshua had and we possess the same Law of the Spirit that John G. Lake had. Under this new law you received when you became born again by His Spirit, disease and sickness has no authority in your body. The only reason the disease or sickness remains is because there is a lack of knowledge. It is permitted there by the confession of your mouth and by acceptance of the disease or sickness. By knowing your rights under the Law of the Spirit, disease does not have a right to be in your body. The problem lies in whether you truly are in agreement with the Law of the Spirit of Knowledge. When you live under the Law of the Spirit, can Satan still try to place disease and sickness on you? He will try because his mission is to kill, steal, and destroy. But once you realize you are now under the Law of the Spirit, you can command the sickness to leave and release healing into your body.

The law of nature says that disease and sickness can kill

the body. The Law of the Spirit through the Spirit of Knowledge says I can command the cancer to leave in the name of Yahshua and it has to go. The law of nature says my bank account is zero and I can't pay the bills but the Law of the Spirit says all riches in Christ are mine. The law of nature says that blind eyes will remain blind, but the Law of the Spirit says lay hands on the sick and they will recover.

When we became born again, our spirits were made new, but our bodies and our souls were not. We need the Spirit of Knowledge to get our bodies and our souls to operate under the Law of the Spirit. How do we get our bodies and our souls to be perfect just like our spirits became perfect when we got saved? There are two ways in which we get our body healed and our soul transformed.

First and foremost, is through the Word of God. The Word of God is creative power. Creator Father did nothing on this earth that He did not first speak. When He spoke it, His voice caused it to happen. That is the power of Yahweh's spoken Word! When our spirits were born again, we were given the same power that Yahweh has – to speak something into being. Jesus taught this principle to His disciples. "For assuredly, I say to you, if you have faith as a mustard seed, you will say to this mountain, 'Move from here to there,' and it will move; and nothing will be impossible for you" (Matthew 17:20). Combining faith with your spoken word will cause things to happen. Combining faith with scriptures declared aloud will cause things to happen. His Word cannot return to Him void. His Word will accomplish what He sent it for and it will prosper in the thing for which he sent it.

The confession of our mouth combined with faith will cause us to operate under the Law of the Spirit. You can never rise above the confession of your mouth! That means you can never excel above what your words are saying about yourself. So what words are you confessing? What are you saying about yourself? Are you telling people you were diagnosed with a disease? Once you confess it, it belongs to you. I am not suggesting going into denial, because the symptoms will tell your body otherwise. But instead of coming into agreement with the enemy's disease, confess with your mouth this disease does not belong to you because "by His stripes you are already healed" (1Peter 2:24). The confession of our mouth has to be consistent and constant! Stop confessing the problem and begin to confess the solution. This is our walk of faith. This is not a naming and claiming it theology where you speak it once and then wait for the answer to manifest. Things will not necessarily happen overnight. With each confession, the solution will move from a mental ascent to heart knowledge. Once it is in your heart, then the solution or healing is ready to happen. Don't give up until you see results.

You can release your perfect spirit into your body for healing because Yahweh's Spirit lives in you. "The spirit of a man will sustain him in sickness" (Proverbs 18:14). Your spirit is perfectly healed and you are under the Law of the Spirit. You can begin to release your healing by saying these words, "I release my perfect spirit into my body and my soul. I command my body and soul to be in submission to my spirit." It is necessary to speak to the spirit of a person regarding healing, do not speak to their body. Most sickness and disease begins in the spirit and then proceeds to the body. Therefore, healing begins in the spirit and proceeds to the body. Addressing spiritual issues can determine the root cause of the illness. Spiritual issues could be hidden or unconfessed sin, emotional toxins such as hatred, anger, and unforgiveness. This is a paradigm shift to the way people have prayed for healing. We are a spirit with a body, not a body with a spirit. "Now may the God of peace Himself sanctify you completely; and may your whole spirit, soul, and body be preserved blameless at the coming of our Lord Jesus Christ. He who calls you is faithful, who also will do it" (1 Thessalonians 5:23).

Through the Spirit of Knowledge, I have come to understand that everyone has a unique electromagnetic field made up of light waves. There are no two the same, just as there are no two fingerprints the same. Yahshua also has a unique electromagnetic field made up of light waves. His light is Healing Light for our spirits, souls, and bodies. His light is brilliant. The apostle Paul experienced Yahshua's brilliant light on the road to Damascus. Many people who have had a divine encounter with Yahshua speak about a brilliant light that fills the room. Yahshua's light is Healing Light. How can I get Yahshua's healing light into my body so I can have divine healing? First, you must come to the realization that the moment you became born again, Yahshua's Spirit entered your spirit and hence your spirit became new. Paul says that we become new creations. I will take this one step further. The moment you became born again, Yahshua's DNA entered into your blood. You now have His DNA flowing through your blood and you already possess His Healing Light. Holy Spirit of Yahweh said this to me.

"My Light is inside you. Let My Light out. The words you speak of Me and through Me are My Light. You have everything you need. You have My Son. Release My Son through your spoken word. Release My Son through My Word. Release My Son through praying in the Spirit. When you pray in tongues, fire comes out of your mouth. Release My Son through your breath. Release My Son through laying on of your hands. Release My Son through

your eyes. Look into people's eyes and see the window to their soul and spirit and release My Son. You carry My glory. Release My glory Light. I have given you scriptural proof that My Son has paid the price for every ailment, sickness, and disease. Use these scriptures to teach people so they can be redeemed fully. Redemption means being free from sin, sickness, pain, unclean spirits, and all the works of Satan. Because of a lack of faith, My children are only preaching a partial redemption. Preach a complete redemptive message which will free people from the curse."

This is the scriptural proof that we have to declare our complete redemption from sin, sickness, pain and any unclean spirits. Declare these healing scriptures out loud.

"Because it is Elohim who said, "Out of darkness Light shall shine," who shone in our hearts to give the brightness of the knowledge of the glory of Yahweh in the face of Yahshua Messiah." (2 Corinthians 4:6 Hebraic Roots Bible)

"Surely He has borne our griefs
And carried our sorrows;
Yet we esteemed Him stricken,
Smitten by God, and afflicted.
But He was wounded for our transgressions,
He was bruised for our iniquities;
The chastisement for our peace was upon Him,
And by His stripes we are healed." (Isaiah 53:4-5)

"Who Himself bore our sins in His own body on the tree, that we, having died to sins, might live for righteousness—by whose stripes you were healed." (1 Peter 2:24)

"Bless the Lord, O my soul,
And forget not all His benefits:
Who forgives all your iniquities,
Who heals all your diseases." (Psalm 103:2)

"And Jesus went about all Galilee, teaching in their synagogues, preaching the gospel of the kingdom, and healing all kinds of sickness and all kinds of disease among the people. Then His fame went throughout all Syria; and they brought to Him all sick people who were afflicted with various diseases and torments, and those who were demon-possessed, epileptics, and paralytics; and He healed them." (Matthew 3:23-24)

CHAPTER SEVEN

The Spirit of The Fear of Yahweh

There are two types of fear. One is from the enemy and places a person in bondage and the other is from Holy Spirit which gives a person a healthy reverence of Yahweh. The unhealthy fear is what most people can relate to at one level or another. This fear can be a spirit of fear, an irrational fear, a fear of the unknown or future, or even a fear of death. I can relate to the spirit of fear because for most of my life I had this spirit. The spirit of fear would rear its ugly head about two weeks before I was set to leave the country on a mission's trip. In the middle of the night I would wake out of a sound sleep and be gripped by fear about the trip. I would pray in the Spirit and the fear would leave. What I was not aware of at the time was this spirit was passed down to me from a previous generation. Since I had this spirit of fear all my life, it was normal for me to have internal fear about situations. Before we were married, my husband called me and said Holy Spirit revealed to him I had the spirit of fear. He cast out the spirit of fear and canceled the generational curse and my life completely shifted. I immediately went from worry and fear to peace and calm. As time went by, I was amazed at the difference in my life because I was now free from fear. Fear from the enemy is designed to rob peace, cause anxiety, and disrupt lives. Fear of Yahweh is just the opposite because it is designed to bring peace, cause joy, and fulfill lives.

"The fear of the Lord is the beginning of wisdom,
And the knowledge of the Holy One is understanding.
For by me your days will be multiplied,
And years of life will be added to you." (Proverbs 9:10-11)

Fear of Yahweh means to have a healthy respect for His position as the one true God of the universe. You show Him respect by giving Him due honor and glory. "Give unto the Lord the glory due to His name; Worship the Lord in the beauty of holiness" (Psalm 29:2). When you know Yahweh as your Papa, you do not fear being judged by Him. He imparts a peace that surpasses all understanding because you are not held accountable for your past sins. Yahshua already took your punishment. You know in your heart that Yahweh is more powerful and mighty than any force in the universe and with Him you are on the winning side. Everyone wants to be a winner. You are guaranteed victory for all eternity with Yahweh and no one but Him can make or keep that promise. When you have a loving reverence for Yahweh and His Son, your life takes on a new dimension. The things of the world that you counted important suddenly shift to being insignificant. Your priorities change when you have a healthy fear and reverence of the Master Creator. Your heart's desire is to please Him, love Him, worship him, and obey Him. We need to cry out for the Spirit of the Fear of Yahweh to be upon us. "Oh, that they had such a heart in them that they would fear Me and always keep all My commandments, that it might be well with them and with their children forever!" (Deuteronomy 5:29). Papa spoke these words to me about the Spirit of Fear of Yahweh.

"My child, I am merciful to those who love Me. My mercy goes from generation to generation to those who have set their heart on Me and love Me. The Spirit of Fear of Yahweh is not about fearing retribution as a result of My judgment. The righteous shall not be judged because My Son took the punishment for all sin. Fear of Yahweh is honoring My position as sovereign Elohim and acknowledging that there are no gods greater than Me. I establish kings and rulers and I remove them at My will. No one can say, 'I did this or I accomplished this on my own.' No man can do anything unless I establish him to perform it. Pride says, 'Look at what I accomplished.' Fear of Yahweh says, 'I am blessed by Yahweh and I am able to accomplish this thing through His power.' Pride says, 'I am powerful and rich and I have a position because of my knowledge.' Fear of Yahweh says, 'Everything I possess is a gift from Yahweh and I am elevated because He decreed it to be so.' Pride says, 'I am better than other people.' Fear of Yahweh says, 'I am nothing without Yahweh.' Pride says, 'There is no God and I am the master of my destiny.' Fear of Yahweh says, 'My soul blesses Yahweh because of all His benefits. Yahweh is the one who forgives all my iniquities and heals all my diseases.' Pride is the opposite of the fear of Yahweh. Pride enslaves. Fear of Yahweh is freedom."

In the Book of Daniel, as a result of his power and wealth, Nebuchadnezzar's heart was lifted up with pride instead of the fear of Yahweh. Yahweh gave him a dream about a large beautiful tree full of fruit. The fruit tree was chopped down at the base, but the roots remained. Daniel interpreted the dream and told

Nebuchadnezzar that he was the tree in the dream. Daniel warned Nebuchadnezzar to repent of his prideful attitude or else Yahweh would make him like a grazing beast of the field. One year after the dream and Daniel's interpretation, Nebuchadnezzar entered his palace in Babylon and bragged that his kingdom was established through his power and for his honor. The words were still coming out of his mouth when Yahweh struck Nebuchadnezzar and he became a lunatic. He was driven out to the field and he ate grass like an ox and remained in an animal-like state for seven years. After seven years were completed, Nebuchadnezzar lifted his head to heaven to acknowledge that Yahweh was the God of the universe. His pride was gone and he was finally humbled. "Now I, Nebuchadnezzar, praise and exalt and honor the King of Heaven, for all His works are truth, and His ways are justice. And He is able to humble those who walk in pride" (Daniel 4:37).

There are times when Yahweh warns people to forsake their pride and fearfully humble themselves before Him. When His warning is repeatedly ignored, He brings His hand of discipline and judgment. Ignorance is no excuse because the Word very boldly proclaims His truth. One biblical truth that has been ignored is that Yahweh gave the land of Israel to David through a covenant. Yahweh established a Salt Covenant with David that gave the control of the land of Israel to him forever. "Should you not know that the Lord God of Israel gave the dominion over Israel to David forever, to him and his sons, by a covenant of salt?" (2 Chronicles 13:5). Through ignorance, the United States is violating the Salt Covenant between Yahweh and Israel. They are violating the covenant by facilitating peace agreements that include dividing Israel's land to make a Palestinian state. There is virtually no fear of Yahweh in the United States government.

"The fear of the Lord is the beginning of knowledge, but fools despise wisdom and instruction" (Proverbs 1:7).

As a result of violating Yahweh's Salt Covenant; salt mines are collapsing in the United States and causing the land to sink. Huge sinkholes all over the United States are happening with such regularity that people are not taking notice anymore. These sinkholes are swallowing up buildings, homes, roads, large parcels of land and in one incident; it swallowed a Florida man in his bed. Experts have no conclusive answer why these sinkholes are appearing with such frequency. Could these sinkholes and salt mine collapses be Yahweh's warning to America? It is a serious matter to ignore a covenant that Yahweh made with David because Yahweh zealously watches over the land He gave to Israel. "A land for which the Lord your God cares; the eyes of the Lord your God are always on it, from the beginning of the year to the very end of the year" (Deuteronomy 11:12).

The United States has been disciplined through various hurricanes, storms, droughts, and floods because of her involvement in dividing Yahweh's land. For the most part, our government remains oblivious to the connection between these disasters and their involvement with Israeli peace negotiations. Here is just one incident where Yahweh has sent His warning about these negotiations. On December 13, 2013 John Kerry was in Israel for negotiations that would give Palestinians an independent state made up of the West Bank, Gaza, and East Jerusalem. That very day, Jerusalem had an unprecedented storm that dropped 20 inches of snow! This is a wakeup call for Israel to stop contemplating giving Yahweh's land as a negotiating tool for peace. The Mayor of Jerusalem even stated that this rare storm was the likes of which we have never seen. Just as Yahweh has given plenty of warning to the United States government, He is also warning the Israeli government to cease using His land as a bargaining tool. "And now, Israel, what does the Lord your God require of you, but to fear the Lord your God, to walk in all His ways and to love Him, to serve the Lord your God with all your heart and with all your soul" (Deuteronomy 10:12). A true fear of Yahweh would cause those in government power to cease with these negotiations.

This is a message I received from Holy Spirit about the United States of America. I do not take these messages lightly, nor do I give them lightly. Carrying a prophetic mantle has not been easy for me because my nature is usually upbeat and I am always looking for the positive and good in situations. When I receive messages like these, my heart becomes heavy for our nation. I was not given a time frame when these events will happen, but it looks like they will occur over a period of time.

"The United States of America is about to swing into a new season. At first it will be a prosperous time, but it will be short lived. Next it will be a season of devastation from all directions. The first devastation will hit and when she is reeling from that one, the next will be right on its heels. When it looks like it cannot get any worse, indeed it will. This series of devastating events will cripple your nation and bring her to her knees. She will realize that she is no longer the powerful nation she once was. Look to the skies and you will see the first devastation. Look to the seas and you will see the next devastation. Look to the earth and you will see the third devastation. I the Lord of the heavens, the earth, and beneath earth have spoken."

There will come a day when all the people of this earth will experience the fear of Yahweh first hand. Those who know Yahshua as Savior will rejoice at His appearing in the sky, but those who do not, will be petrified. The sky will roll back like a scroll and Yahshua will appear. If you have not made a decision to wholeheartedly follow Yahshua prior to His appearing, you will be one who is filled with dread and fear of Yahweh. This event will surely happen and we are closer than most people realize. Prepare yourself, because He is coming very, very soon. The scoffers will remain scoffers until that great day of the Lord.

> "And the kings of the earth, the great men, the rich men, the commanders, the mighty men, every slave and every free man, hid themselves in the caves and in the rocks of the mountains, and said to the mountains and rocks, "Fall on us and hide us from the face of Him who sits on the throne and from the wrath of the Lamb! For the great day of His wrath has come, and who is able to stand?" (Revelation 6:15-18)

> "The earth quakes before them,
> The heavens tremble;
> The sun and moon grow dark,
> And the stars diminish their brightness.
> The Lord gives voice before His army,
> For His camp is very great;
> For strong is the One who executes His word.
> For the day of the Lord is great and very terrible;
> Who can endure it?" (Joel 2: 10-11)

Conclusion

We are in desperate need of the Seven Spirits of Yahweh to complete the mission of the body of Christ before Yahshua returns. I had a spiritual dream that sums up the current condition of the organized church today. There was a large wedding party proceeding down the aisle of a church. The wedding party had many bridesmaids that filled the entire length of the aisle. The bridesmaids were walking down the aisle to the front of the church and the first bridesmaid suddenly began to stumble and she fell backwards. When she fell, she hit into the bridesmaid behind her, who also fell, until the entire procession fell backwards like dominoes. I ran to the back of the church to make sure the bride did not fall, but by the time I got there, she was already knocked down. Embarrassed by the fiasco, the entire bridal party got off the floor and went to the back of the church to regroup. They proceeded down the aisle once again. In the dream, I prayed in tongues as the bridal party began their procession so they would not stumble and fall again. This was the Lord's message regarding this dream.

"My bride the church is stumbling and falling. Stop playing church. I hold this against the leaders of churches and

ministries. Stop fleecing My sheep. You have made religion a business and you are no different than the Pharisees. Money and possessions have become more important than the souls of people. You have led people down a broad road that leads to hell. Narrow is the way and few find it. I am calling My true followers to come out of Babylon. Come out of the religious system that is manmade and leads to destruction. Follow Me with all your heart and you will see salvation. Without holiness, you will not enter into the Kingdom of Light. Forsake your wicked ways and wholeheartedly obey My commands. My bride needs to pray in the Spirit in tongues so I can strengthen her and reveal to her. I am coming very soon. Prepare yourself."

One of the reasons the church is stumbling and falling is because denominations have divided the body of Christ. Every denomination has some error mixed with its truth. The error has become a hindrance to unity within the body of Christ. Some Baptist churches believe the spiritual gifts ended at the end of the apostolic age and they are not for today. The Presbyterian Church USA is ordaining homosexuals. The Methodists do not believe in the gifts of the Spirit and are also ordaining homosexuals. The Catholics teach that purgatory is an alternative place for hell, if people don't make it to heaven. The Lutherans believe that infant baptisms work for forgiveness of sins, deliver from death and the devil, and gives eternal salvation. The Assembly of God is prideful and thinks they have spiritually arrived because they have the baptism of the Holy Spirit. The Christian Missionary Alliance does not acknowledge that women are called into the Five Fold ministry and one should not seek the gifts of Holy Spirit. The Church of Jesus Christ of Latter Day Saints does not believe that Jesus is God. The Jehovah Witnesses do not acknowledge Jesus as the Messiah.

How can all these denominations, which profess Christianity, walk in such error? They have become organizations instead of the body of Christ and they stopped seeking His truth. Yahshua is the way, the truth, and the life. Yahshua is the Word made flesh. If you desire His truth, start studying His Word and ask for His truth. This is a season when truth is imperative. Every religious denomination has some error and it is time to ask Holy Spirit to reveal these wrong doctrines. There are those who would rather hold onto error because they find their identity in their denomination. Yahshua warned us in scripture about those whose identities are wrapped up in religion instead of a relationship with Him.

> "Not everyone who says to Me, 'Lord, Lord,' shall enter the kingdom of heaven, but he who does the will of My Father in heaven. Many will say to Me in that day, 'Lord, Lord, have we not prophesied in Your name, cast out demons in Your name, and done many wonders in Your name?' And then I will declare to them, 'I never knew you; depart from Me, you who practice lawlessness!" (Matthew 7:21-23)

Which Jesus do you follow? Do you follow the Jesus of the Baptist who deny His power, the Jesus of the Presbyterians and Methodists who are ordaining homosexuals, the Jesus of the Catholics who elevate Mary as co-Redeemer, the Jesus of the Lutherans who profess infant baptism is salvation, the Jesus of the Mormons who deny He is the Messiah, the Jesus of the Jehovah Witnesses who call Holy Spirit a force, the Jesus of the Assembly of God who have spiritual pride, the Jesus of the Christian Missionary Alliance good ole boys club, or any other Jesus associated with a denomination?

I don't follow any of those Jesus'. As a matter of fact, Jesus is not His real name. The letter "J" was not in the English language until 1634. If the letter "J" did not exist until 1634, then how could His birth name be Jesus? The truth is that His Hebrew name is Yahshua. The Greeks translated Yahshua's name to Iesous which later became Jesus when the letter "J" was added to the English alphabet. One day I was talking to Yahshua about His name and I asked Him this question.

"How is it that You honored a name that was not Yours for so many centuries?" Yahshua answered me.

"It was My Essence and My Light that broke through. Child, you got saved under the name of Jesus, but it was not the name, but My Essence attached to the name. I am glad that you know Me and use My given name and you are teaching people truth."

Then I asked Yahshua this question because I wanted to absolutely please Him.

"What do you prefer to be called my precious Savior, Jesus or Yahshua?" He quickly responded to me this way.

"What do you prefer to be called, Pat or Patricia?"

I answered Him, "I prefer Patricia, but I will answer to Pat." Then Yahshua responded.

"It is the same with Me child. I prefer Yahshua, but I will answer to Jesus."

I choose to call the Son of Yahweh by the name He prefers because Yahshua is the name he was given at birth. You can decide for yourself. The Spirit of Yahweh is purging old religious ways in these last days and ushering in His truth through the Seven Spirits of Yahweh.

Impartation

Prayer of Salvation

If you have never taken the opportunity to become a child of Yahweh, now is the time. Don't delay, today is the day of your salvation. If you died right now and you don't know whether you would go to heaven or hell, then you need Yahshua. He paid the price for all your wrong doings by being tortured to death on the cross. Yahshua rose from the dead on the third day and He is alive and is seated at the right hand of Yahweh. Yahshua's shed blood is the only way to have your relationship with Father Yahweh restored and made right, so you can have eternal life in heaven. It does not matter what you have done in the past. There is no wickedness, depravity, or immoral thing too big to be forgiven. Set it in your heart right now that you want to turn away from your old life so you can have a new beginning. This is the day you can be free from drugs, alcohol, cigarettes, pornography, formication, adultery, homosexuality, anger, despair, anxiety, fear, rejection, sickness, disease, unforgiveness, and self-condemnation. This is the day you can have complete freedom in Christ! This is the day you can be forgiven of all your wrongdoings and have a clean slate to begin fresh. If this is truly your desire, then say this simple prayer with a sincere heart.

"Dear Father Yahweh, I am through running from You. I admit that I have committed wrong acts in my life which have separated me from You. It is my desire to turn from all of these evil things and I ask You to forgive me. I believe in my heart that Your Son Yahshua paid the price for my sins by dying on the cross and by His stripes I am healed. I believe in my heart that Yahshua rose from the dead on the third day and he is alive and is seated at Your right hand. Adopt me as your child today and write my name in the lamb's Book of Life."

If you just prayed the prayer, your spirit is now new and you have a direct line of communication to Yahshua and Yahweh. You can ask Him anything and he hears you because you are His child. He wants you to talk to Him every day about your life. Your name is recorded in heaven and today is your spiritual birthday. Heaven is your eternal destination. You have been set free from sin, all bondages, sickness, and disease. Today is just the beginning of all these changes in your new life. Yahweh has so much more for you, but you must do your part. If you do not have a bible, you need to get one and begin reading it. You need to spend time talking to Yahweh and Yahshua like He is your best friend, because He is. You also need the other impartations in this book to equip you spiritually. I am so proud of you for making this very important decision for salvation.

Prayer of Forgiveness

In all my ministry years, I have found the biggest obstacle to receiving an impartation of the baptism of Holy Spirit and the Seven Spirits of Yahweh is unforgiveness. The opposite of love is unforgiveness because it breeds hatred and bitterness. Bitterness is a result of unforgiveness that has festered over time. Bitter people are angry on the inside and their anger manifests on the outside. Love and forgiveness is the cure for your internal turmoil and Yahshua wants to set you free.

Yahshua is Yahweh's love personified. He came to this earth to display His Father's love. Yahshua's entire purpose for coming was to forgive mankind so there could be restoration in the love relationship between Yahweh and man. Forgiveness was manifested on the cross when Yahshua spoke these words. "Father forgive them, for they know not what they are doing." It could also be paraphrased this way. "Father, love them for they know not what they are doing." Forgiveness and love are synonymous. They are the same. You need to forgive everyone for everything. No exceptions!

Forgiveness does not mean that you will trust that person again, especially if the offense was great. Forgiveness does not mean you have to be best friends with your offender. Forgiveness simply means you no longer hold that person accountable for what they have done to you. Forgiveness means you let go of the offense and you stop talking about it to others. There is freedom in forgiveness and bondage in unforgiveness.

Unforgiveness breeds hatred, anger and bitterness and is the open door for sickness and disease to enter the body. Unforgiveness is a spiritual sickness that leads to physical sickness.

This is the reason many people are emotionally and physically sick. Yahshua became our substitute on the cross to take the punishment for our sin to bare all of our sickness and disease. It was on the cross that we received the forgiveness of all our sin and healing for our bodies. Forgiveness and healing go hand in hand. You cannot separate them.

Unforgiveness also closes the door to receive the blessing of Yahweh. If you have any unforgiveness for any one, you will not be able to receive the blessings of these impartations. Take the time right now and bow your head and ask Yahshua to place the forgiveness in your heart for all your offenders. Tell Yahshua you no longer hold that person accountable for what they have done to you and tell Him you choose to forgive them. Tell Yahshua that you choose to forgive yourself for anything you have done because He has forgiven you. Right now, out loud, name your offenders and their offenses against you and say,

"I choose to forgive (Place their name here) for this offense (Name the offense). I choose to forgive myself for (Place the situation or thing you feel guilty about here)."

Prayer of Freedom

The next step in receiving the Baptism of Holy Spirit and the Seven Spirits of Yahweh is to be clean of everything that is not pure and holy. When we have an empty vessel, He can fill us completely. By declaring the Word Warrior's Freedom Prayer out loud, you are preparing your vessel to receive the impartations.

The Word Warrior's Freedom Prayer

" Almighty YAHWEH, I honor You as the Lord God of Abraham, Isaac and Jacob. I ask You to forgive me of my sins through Your son's sacrifice. I trust He was born of a virgin, lived a sinless life, was crucified and rose from the dead on the third day to sit and rule beside You in heaven.

I REJECT every thought, idea, concept, intent, desire or spirit in me that does not glorify you in the name of Your Son, YAHSHUA!

I REBUKE every thought, idea, concept, intent, desire or spirit in me that does not glorify you in the name of Your Son, YAHSHUA!

Lord God Almighty, You REBUKE every thought, idea, concept, intent, desire or spirit from me that does not glorify you in the name of Your Son, YAHSHUA!

Father YAHWEH, send down your consuming FIRE to burn every residue of evil thought, idea, concept, intent, desire or spirit out of me in the name of Your Son, YAHSHUA, right now at this very moment!

Fill me Spirit of YAHWEH to overflow with Your LOVE and Your FIRE. I thank you my Father, for what you are doing and what you have done in me in Your Son's Holy name, so it is written, so it is."

Impartation of the Baptism of Holy Spirit

I have been instructed by Yahweh to impart the Baptism of His Holy Spirit and He has graciously given me the anointing to accomplish this. Everyone I have prayed for that truly wanted to received it, is now speaking in tongues. I have imparted the Baptism of His Holy Spirit all over the world. I have imparted the gift of tongues to people in India, Africa, Israel, on airplanes, by the Sea of Galilee, in church settings, public parks, and many more places. I have imparted to children as young as 7 years old and they have received a prayer language. If you truly desire to receive the Baptism of Holy Spirit and receive your prayer language, then continue reading and follow the instructions.

The Baptism of Holy Spirit is to empower you as a witness for Yahshua to take His gospel everywhere you go. This Baptism is also for equipping Yahweh's flock for the work of the ministry. There are spiritual gifts that Holy Spirit has for each believer.

"There are diversities of gifts, but the same Spirit. There are differences of ministries, but the same Lord. And there are diversities of activities, but it is the same God who works all in all. But the manifestation of the Spirit is given to each one for the profit of all: for to one is given the word of wisdom through the Spirit, to another the word of knowledge through the same Spirit to another faith by the same Spirit, to another gifts of healings by the same Spirit, to another the working of miracles, to another prophecy, to another discerning of spirits, to another different kinds of tongues, to another the interpretation of tongues. But one and the same Spirit works all these things, distributing to each one individually as He wills." (1 Corinthians 12:4-11)

Before I give you His instructions how to receive the Baptism of His Holy Spirit, you must understand that speaking in tongues is a verbal gift from Holy Spirit. That means you must engage your mouth and your voice when you are receiving your prayer language. When I instruct you to place your hand on your cheek, you may feel your mouth tremble and your lips quiver. If they do not, that is alright. What will happen is that your mouth will begin to move with unknown syllables that sound foreign. At this point, you MUST place a voice to these syllables because that is your unique prayer language. The biggest mistake people make when they are on the verge of getting their prayer language is to think that Holy Spirit will take control of their mouth. Therefore, they don't know they have to open their mouth to speak. Holy Spirit never controls any part of your body! You must submit your tongue to Holy Spirit and He prays through you in an unknown spiritual language which is a perfect prayer language known only to Yahweh.

If you want to receive the Baptism of His Holy Spirit to speak in tongues; then place your left hand on this page and lay your right hand on the side of your cheek. Speak these words out loud while your left hand is on these words and on your right hand is on your cheek,

"In the Name of Yahshua I command the spirit of fear, spirit of doubt, spirit of unbelief, and any religious spirit to leave me and get out, now!"

"Holy Spirit, I submit my mouth to You. Holy Spirit, pray through me right now in Your spiritual language."

Holy Spirit is now passing through these words into your body! Keep your left hand on these words and your right hand on your cheek. Relax your jaw and open your mouth and say out loud, "Ahhhhhhhh." Now that you have activated your voice, you will begin to form unknown syllables with your tongue and lips. Don't think about the words you are forming because they are coming through your spirit, not your mind. Remember to keep your voice speaking as you form the syllables with your tongue.

The syllables you hear coming out of your mouth is your unique prayer language. Don't be discouraged if you only hear a few syllables and they sound like gibberish. Keep speaking them and your prayer language will increase. The more time you spend using your prayer language the more it will increase. Congratulations! You have just received the Baptism of Holy Spirit and you also received spiritual gifts that are listed in 1 Corinthians Chapter 12.

Impartation of the Seven Spirits of Yahweh

~ The Spirit of Yahweh ~

~ The Spirit of Wisdom ~

~ The Spirit of Understanding ~

~ The Spirit of Counsel ~

~ The Spirit of Might ~

~ The Spirit of Knowledge ~

~ The Spirit of the Fear of Yahweh ~

Yahshua had the fullness of the Spirit of Yahweh to operate in the great signs, wonders, and miracles. If we expect to operate in the same power as Yahshua, then we need the fullness of the Seven Spirits of Yahweh. Yahshua made a bold statement when He said we would do greater works then He did. "Most assuredly, I say to you, he who believes in Me, the works that I do he will do also; and greater works than these he will do, because I go to My Father" (John 14:12). Yahshua spoke that statement before the cross, but He could see down through ages into future generations. Before the cross, no one had salvation through Yahshua. After the cross, salvation was available to all who totally relied on Him and His completed work on the cross. Yahshua's disciples and future generations of disciples would become His instruments to bring His gospel to people so they could be saved. Salvation is the greater work we have a part in that Yahshua spoke about because salvation is truly the greatest miracle of all!

Yahweh has instructed me to impart His Seven Spirits to spiritually equip His children. If you are serious about being an ambassador of Yahshua and you have a burning desire to see souls birthed into the kingdom of heaven and you want to operate in signs, wonders and miracles, then you need the fullness of the Seven Spirits of Yahweh.

Once again, Holy Spirit has revealed to me that there is a very powerful anointing upon the words in this book. If you want to receive the Seven Spirits of Yahweh so you can operate in the fullness of His Spirits, then place your left hand over these words and place your right hand on your forehead and speak these words.

"I receive the Seven Spirits of Yahweh to operate in signs, wonders, and miracles. I receive the Spirit of Yahweh, the Spirit of Wisdom, the Spirit of Understanding, the Spirit of Counsel, the Spirit of Might, the Spirit of Knowledge, and the Spirit of the Fear of Yahweh."

By speaking those words, you have activated your faith. His anointing is upon you and you have received the fullness of the Seven Spirits of Yahweh. You have just entered a deeper dimension of the revelations of Yahweh and He will reveal things that you could not possibly know without the fullness of His Spirit. You will begin to notice that you are now more sensitive to happenings in the spiritual realm. You will hear Yahweh's voice more clearly and consistently. You are equipped to be His warrior to be on the front line of battle. You will see results that are astounding! Just remember to remain humble because it is His power through the Seven Spirits of Yahweh. Glorify and magnify Yahweh for the marvelous works He is about to accomplish through you.

~ I thank you precious Yahweh for Your Seven Spirits and for Your glorious presence upon all those who have read this book and received. ~

Your Handmaiden,
Patricia.

Contact the Author

Dr. Patricia Green is the author of several books and a much sought-after international conference speaker. Dr Patricia has a passion for souls and seeing new converts empowered to reach a lost and dying world for our Lord and Savior, YAHSHUA.

Dr. Patricia carries a special anointing to impart the Baptism into Holy Spirit of Yahweh and to impart the Seven Spirits of Yahweh found in Isaiah 11:2.

Dr. Patricia has imparted the Baptism into Holy Spirit of Yahweh to many pastors and their spouses along with the Seven Spirits of Yahweh.

Her special anointing is leading multitudes to the cross of YAHSHUA which she has done through speaking engagements and her second book, *Heaven or Hell...Your Choice*.

Dr. Patricia and her husband travel as a team and are available to teach and impart spiritual gifts to congregations and conferences nationally and internationally as the Spirit of Yahweh leads. A schedule of events is available on her website.

Dr Patricia and her husband personally attend to every prayer request.

For more information, please contact the author.
www.DrPatricia.com

Need
additional
copies?

To order more copies of

THE SEVEN SPIRITS
of YAHWEH

contact CertaPublishing.com

❐ Order online at:
   CertaPublishing.com/Bookstore

❐ Call 855-77-CERTA or

❐ Email Info@CertaPublishing.com

Additional Book Available by
Dr. Patricia Green

❏   Order online at:
     CertaPublishing.com/Bookstore

❏   Call 855-77-CERTA or

❏   Email Info@CertaPublishing.com

Additional Book Available by
Dr. Patricia Green

Dr. Patricia Green

I AM
THE
GOD
THAT
REVEALS

Unveiling of Revelation

❏ Order online at:
   CertaPublishing.com/Bookstore

❏ Call 855-77-CERTA or

❏ Email Info@CertaPublishing.com

Additional Book Available by
Dr. Patricia Green

Dr. Patricia Green

Heaven
OR Hell
...Your Choice

Unveiling Divine Revelations

❒ Order online at:
CertaPublishing.com/Bookstore

❒ Call 855-77-CERTA or

❒ Email Info@CertaPublishing.com

Additional Book Available by
Dr. Patricia Green

❒   Order online at:
    CertaPublishing.com/Bookstore

❒   Call 855-77-CERTA or

❒   Email Info@CertaPublishing.com